FILICIDE

THE MYTHIC REALITY OF CHILDHOOD

DOUGLAS MILBURN

i

Lovis Corinth: *The Great Martyrdom* (1907).

For M.W.S. and her progeny:
May they be fruitful and multiply.

CONTENTS

Children are still terrae incognitae.
—Novalis.

If, as seems more and more likely, the future judges ours to have been primarily an age of exploration, we will then be rightly celebrated for the wide range of our curiosity. At the same time we will be wondered at for our failure to explore in detail certain proximate areas. Paramount among these would have to be childhood.

Not that we have been totally remiss. We have produced clever, even admirable works about children, running the gamut from theoretical studies (Reich) to empirical studies (Piaget) and practical studies (Dr. Spock). We have even on occasion found room for children in our art, though not very often. And—cries the educationist from the back row—don't forget the volumes and volumes on pedagogy. Indeed, let us not forget the schoolmasters and schoolmarms, for it is truly into their hands that we have delivered the children.

Yes, books about children we have in great number. *Filicide* is a book about children from a curious perspective, namely that of an adult who has attempted to see and interpret history from the child's perspective while using adult abilities to describe and articulate the child's perceptions. The result is a book unlike most of our books about children in that it is heavily biased in favor of children. This bias may cause certain problems for the adult reader, since we are so accustomed to having things our way. The argument from childhood, for example, produces a number of unusual skirmishes with several of the most beloved idols of our age (rationality and science, to name two), the outcome of which is a series of judgments of adult behavior at the heart of the book. These judgments may at first strike the adult reader as outrageous, or hectoring, or both.

The territory out of which I have tried to speak here—the world of children—is, as Novalis observed, peculiarly unknown to us. We were after all once children ourselves. It is a world which is congruent with ours in time and space and which appears to share many of the same values. But how rarely and poorly we remember that world. It is perhaps less saccharine and surely more profound than we would have it be in our social imagery. The indirect route I have chosen to get into that world—that of myth—leads one into a topsy-turvy world where many of our most treasured truths turn out to be self-serving adult assumptions designed to shore up this rather shaky version of reality which we call civilization.

If my formulations of the outrage of children are improperly outrageous, then I have spoken poorly in their stead. The children's words, if they could ever get our attention, would surely ring true no matter how outrageous the content. If my tone has in places become hectoring, then I have succumbed to the temptation of ideological argument. The children would surely speak with the natural force of long affliction.

The book grew out of my own experience as child and adult, as son and father—experience which, I should note here, is not as negative as some readers might assume from the following pages. Observing my behavior as a father, I became curious to understand and eager to correct certain differences between my conscious intentions toward my children and my actual behavior. Initially my thinking was influenced and encouraged by the women's movement. For quite some time I thought I was writing a men's liberation book, or some such thing. I eventually realized that to write that sort of book in this patriarchy, one has to define one's masculine self in terms of the oppression of women. While there is much to be said for the cathartic effect of a proper mea culpa, that approach yielded only partial answers to the widespread problem of adult hypocrisy toward children. I had nowhere left to look but to the common heritage we all share beneath our sex roles, namely, childhood.

What began parochially as a book of men's liberation became, presumptuously perhaps, a book of children's liberation and then, surprisingly, a book about the sources of human suffering and certain possibilities for release. Through it all the child's perspective prevailed. The review of history from that perspective produced several unexpected, rich juxtapositions. These range from an illumination of the way in which the two sex roles are more alike than they are different, to an unusual view of the nature of the interior conflict which informs and possibly creates what what we think of as personality.

Given the nature of my thesis, the multiplication of examples presented an even larger problem than usual. The myths discussed are intended to be not exhaustive but suggestive. The reader whose interest is piqued will be able to generate additional examples at will. Only one work is missing which I would like to have been able to include. The proper explication of Anne Rice's extraordinary novel, *Interview with the Vampire*—which I believe can be given the same sort of close, filicidal reading which I give an earlier "horror" novel here, must await someone with a more profound feminist experience than my own.

It may seem that I have (childishly?) ignored or undervalued various aspects of the culture which are important to us adults. For example, the name Bach will not be found in *Filicide*, though there are passages of cultural critique which may at first strike the reader as excessively negative and where some reference to the accomplishments of the past is called for. Some, perhaps many, adults derive great solace from Bach as they make their way through a difficult world. If I have not mentioned Bach and other comparable figures, it is because in a world seen through child's eyes, Bach offers precious little solace. And the adult in me is left to ask: what of comparable power and beauty and sustenance has this culture created where children may reliably expect to find solace? The possible answers—this or that fairy tale, this or that religious celebration, this or that intelligent television pro-gram—when considered carefully indicate something of the degree of adult bias in the culture. More important, that sort of question can lead us into an under-standing of children very much at odds with the most traditional as well as the most enlightened views of the lost world which they, and perhaps we too, still inha-bit.

INTRODUCTION

A crucifixion, a fixing to a cross (see p. iii). Where is this cross? We can see only that it is supported by a wall. We cannot tell whether it is outdoors or indoors, though the lighting suggests an interior scene. No dramatic, windswept mountaintop here. Somewhere, four men attach a fifth man to a cross.

And where is the crowd of spectators, where are the curious idlers, the anguished friends, where is the grieving mother? Where are the angels? Where is the thunder, the lightning? How is it that nature does not rise to protest this crucifixion?

And this is hardly the face that will plead forgiveness for the crucifiers on the basis that they are ignorant of what they are doing. This face reveals only terror and pain as a hammer drives a spike through a foot. Nor is this the face that will look at fellow victims on adjacent crosses and assure them that they will shortly be reunited in paradise. It is the face of terrified isolation. We can see no other crosses, no fellow martyrs.

The four men—the crucifiers—how they cooperate. The logistics of crucifixion requires a certain amount of cooperation. The victim must be held in position as the arms are tied to the cross, then held again as the feet are nailed, and then the hands. One can see the need for cooperation. Do we not also perceive a certain spirit of camaraderie, as if these four have done this before, many times perhaps?

One of them—is he the foreman?—stands back thoughtfully, almost disinterested but slightly amused by the group's handiwork. He judges, much as a mason would step back to check a partly finished wall, or an artist, to contemplate a painting in progress. His expression indicates it may not be the best of jobs but it will do.

What blasphemy is this? Where is the covering, the loincloth? Who would look at the male organ of a man or a god at the height of his passion? Yet there it is, occupying the center of composition of the painting. The eye tries to avoid it, but the lines of force draw us irresistibly to that point.

Many questions. As a culture, how do we get to crucifixion at all, especially a crucifixion which becomes the chief symbol of a major religion? And how do we get from that bloody atonement for universal sin to Lovis Corinth's elemental, secular crucifixion painted in 1907? How is it that such an act came to occupy the conscious or unconscious center of so many lives, indeed of an entire civilization? Is it an accident that the civilization that centered on crucifixion as its primary mythic act should have become the dominant planetary civilization? It is very peculiar that the most sacred image of a civilization as diverse and creative as this one should be that of a man nailed to a cross, and even more peculiar that we should perceive the crucified one as a son.

The question becomes: who is being crucified and what is the actual relationship of the crucified one to the rest of us? We know that the central figure in the modern Western pantheon is a crucified male deity. We further know that he has a filial relationship with us, by all reports. But why a *crucified* god? And why the role of son for that god? An image forms. The mind's eye looks away—was the image that of a crucified child?

Whatever the meaning of this odd act called crucifixion, it is clearly an act of violence. We begin then with violence.

2. THE DISCRIMINATION OF VIOLENCES

Violence is interference; interference, violence. In the strictest sense, we cannot exist without being violent. We inhabit a continuum of physical violence—from the most basic and minimal of interferences such as breathing and occupying physical space, through the more obviously violent acts of assault, rape, and murder, to the ultimate, sometimes planetary, violence known as war.

We also inhabit a continuum of behavioral violence, that being interference with another person in some suasive, manipulative way. Words form our most common means of behavioral violence. Money is a highly effective weapon of behavioral violence. But our most potent method of behavioral violence lies in the exemplary force of our lives as we live them. The nature and quality of our lives reflect and advertise our conscious and unconscious decisions in a highly convincing, highly visible manner.

The behavioral ideal of "nonviolence" is thus a nonexistent category, describing as it does a state which we cannot achieve this side of death. The nonviolent person is understood to be one who will neither use nor resist physical violence. Few would deny that that is a noble and possibly even valuable behavior for a human being to aspire to. The doctrine of nonviolence is based on the attractive but dangerously naive assumption that all violence is physical, that is, bloody. While we in this century can certainly qualify as experts on bloodshed with our hundred million war deaths, we also qualify equally well as experts on the techniques of behavioral violence with our rapid and continuing development of the various kinds of propaganda—commercial, political, artistic, scientific, educational, and religious.

Our choice then is not between violence and nonviolence. The choice is far subtler, and is one we all make whether we are aware of it or not; namely, at what level of violence we will exist, what level of violence we find acceptable. We make the choice as individuals and then, cumulatively, as cultures. We learn, in other words, the discrimination of violences.

In making that choice, a further discrimination occurs. Again whether we are aware of it or not, we discriminate between natural violence and contrived violence. Natural violence consists of those acts of interference which we cannot avoid— breathing, occupying space, and so on. Contrived violence consists of all other acts of interference. The quality of life which an individual or a society enjoys is largely a result of the kinds of contrived violence perceived as acceptable. One American age finds its values and its frustrations best represented by baseball—a later age obtains satisfaction from football.

The positive side of historical progress consists of our increasing sensitivity to and refinement of the discrimination of violences. As that process occurs we find that those forms of violence which we think of, unconsciously or consciously, as natural diminish in number. We come to perceive that various kinds of violence which we once thought inevitable ("human nature") are in fact contrived. We become aware that we have gentler choices in vast areas of our behavior where we once thought we either had no choices at all or only the choice between different kinds of more or less brutal violence. It is possible that the American experience in Vietnam represents an extension of the semantic discrimination of violences into the world of physical behavior. After a prolonged internal struggle, American civilization realized it could no longer accept the validity of certain ancient justifications concerning the unavoidability, the naturalness if you will, of international violence.

A similar growth in the discrimination of violences may be seen throughout history in the area of human rights. One by one, the old arguments in support of the political, legal, religious, and sexist exploitation of groups and individuals fall as we become more aware of the extent to which we can determine and act on acceptable limits to our violence.

Now we come to speak of children and their role in the system of contrived violence. We have long assumed that the violence we perpetrate on children is either natural (unavoidable) or necessary (*We're doing this for your own good*). Growing awareness of cultural relativism has undercut that assumption to some extent. The most basic part of the pedagogical assumption, namely that the child is the property of and is totally given to the power of the parents or their legal surrogates, remains in full force throughout the planet, in societies of every political stripe. Massive, maximum interference in the child's development and growth is still the order of the day in even the most enlightened societies—however one may choose to define enlightened. Children, the only true mirrors available to us, remain the true slave class, as they have been from the beginning of history.

Progress in the area of children's rights has not been entirely lacking. Infanticide, once common to societies in all parts of the world, is now illegal in the more civilized countries. Many nations now have laws designed to protect the child from the more extreme forms of physical abuse; but note that we continue to define child abuse rather narrowly. Child beating in the form of paddling, spanking, or whipping continues to be a generally accepted, indeed popular, form of pedagogy in both homes and schools throughout the world.

Only recently have we begun studying the history of childhood. A very large part of that study must be the long and bloody record of the child as physically abused slave. Of the behavioral violence to which we subject children we have hardly begun to speak at all. Modern ideological and quasi-religious movements have made some attempt to analyze our behavioral violence toward children; but the insights generated by, for example, Marxism on the one hand or psychoanalysis on the other are very much adult-oriented, aimed primarily at the solution of adult problems, with the problems of children receiving attention mostly to the extent that they contribute to adult difficulties.

The whole process of acculturation—to which every child is subjected—is an act of contrived violence. For a very long time we have believed, to the extent that we thought about the process at all, that it was either natural (child as property) or necessary *(Honor thy father and thy mother)*. As we have begun to question the "naturalness" of masculinity and femininity, we also begin to question the naturalness of childhood as we have experienced it for thousands of years. If sex roles— the foundations of our adult, civilized personalities—are mutable, then we conclude that those roles as we know then, as we are them, are imposed on us as children. The "natural" violence of traditional masculinity and femininity is revealed as the contrived violence of humanity, perpetrated—innocently perhaps but no less violent for being innocently done—on every generation of children.

7

II. FILICIDE

filicide. 1. The literal or figurative killing of one's son or daughter. 2. One who thus kills one's son or daughter. 3. A son or daughter thus killed by his or her parent or parents.

1. THE THEORY OF FILICIDE

Filicide is a universal crime in this civilization. As children, we are all victims of filicide. As adults, we are all perpetrators of filicide. Through behavioral example, psychological coercion, and physical force, fathers and mothers impose on sons a behavioral role called "masculinity" and on daughters a behavioral role called "femininity." These two roles so effectively constrain and determine the lives of sons and daughters that the result is a living death, a lifelong comatose existence. The two roles shut off vast areas of human potential and growth. The imposition of the son role is thus son-murder: filicide. The imposition of the daughter-role is thus daughter-murder: filicide.

Filicide is the primary formative experience of the son and the daughter and largely determines the reactive standards by which the grown-up son, called "father," and the grown-up daughter, called "mother," lead their lives and in turn commit filicide on the next generation of children. Filicidal behavior is an unspoken norm by which society and human reality are shaped, perceived, and judged by all members of society.

Filicide occurs in what we may call the proto-scene, that being the moment when the parent exerts and confirms its control of the son or daughter and the moment when the son or daughter, to survive, yields to that control by beginning to adopt the appropriate masculine or feminine behavior. The proto-scene is the true moment of birth for the fear-based self which will grow into the adult personality and which one comes to think of as "oneself." The proto-scene may be brief and intense or it may be extended over a period of months or years during infancy and childhood.

Whatever the surface differences between "masculine" behavior and "feminine" behavior, the two roles are generated by the same experience—filicide—and are at bottom nothing more than two adaptations to that experience. They appear to be quite different. We divide the allowable areas of behavior into the two roles: masculine equals dominant, active, rational, war-making, etc.—everything conjured in our minds by the words "man," or "father"; feminine equals submissive, passive, emotional, homemaking, etc.—everything conjured in our minds by the words "woman," or "mother." (The bias in this civilization is, obviously, patriarchal; a matriarchal society would be characterized by different emphases.)

Beneath the apparent differences between us as masculine and feminine creatures

11

lies our shared experience of filicide. The nature of that experience and of our two sex roles is determined by the following factors:

- The behavioral and physical violence used to impose the sex roles.
- The implicit, total rejection of the child as an independent entity responsible for the creation of its own personality and for the deeds it commits.
- The universal amnesia among victims and perpetrators concerning the actual deed itself, as well as the unconsciousness of the father and mother as they commit filicide.
- The emotional relationship between perpetrator (parent) and victim (son or daughter).
- The respective ages and physical sizes of the perpetrator (adult) and the victim (infant or child).

The theory of filicide is a description of our behavior toward children in terms of what we actually do, as opposed to what we think—and claim—we do. Our adult posturings toward children range from the primitive *(I'm doing this for your own good;* or: *This hurts me as much as it hurts you)* to the somewhat less primitive *("freedom, not license")*. Such posturings may at one time have had some survival value. If we remove them now, we find we are left with the brutal reality of filicide as the hidden foundation of our attitudes toward children.

The perception of the behavior came first, then the label. The word, filicide, was not chosen lightly. It is a harsh word for a harsh reality and a tragic truth about ourselves which we have through the centuries attempted to hide and disguise in a thousand clever and not-so-clever ways. It is as if we are, as children, put to sleep; many of us remain then contentedly asleep through our adult lives, unaware of the unexplored potential within us all. Some glimpse that potential and then spend years trying to wake up, that being the first step, which must be taken, before growth again becomes possible.

The implications of the theory of filicide extend from immediate questions of pedagogy and child-rearing into many areas of adult behavior toward adults. Several of the major myths and systems of religious belief in our culture are, it turns out, thoroughly grounded in this extraordinary behavior which I call "filicide." Examining those myths and beliefs, it becomes apparent that, as history has progressed, we have been at pains to find some satisfactory way to justify our hidden, on-going, compulsive filicidal behavior.

12

To survey briefly territory which we shall cover shortly in more detail: the Oedipus myth takes on new meaning in the light of the theory of filicide. Freud, who gave us our modern reading of the story, ignores the curious fact that the first major event in Oedipus' life is his parents' attempt to kill him—a fact which will enable us to turn the Freudian reading topsy-turvy. In another area: the Judeo-Christian tradition begins with an extreme case of behavioral filicide. God rejects his newly created children, Adam and Eve, as unworthy of him and of his paradise. That tradition continues with Abraham, who becomes a willing and conscious perpetrator of fili-cide—though the deity stops him short of the actual murder of Isaac.

So deep and great is our guilt concerning our actual behavior toward our children, it seems we could not rest until we had elevated the justification of filicide to the highest possible level, an attainment which Christianity achieves: God sends his son to earth and kills him. And we then choose to see the crucifixion of Jesus, the son of man and also known as the son of God, not only as a good thing but as the best thing that ever happened. For a millennium and a half that cosmically filicidal interpretation of the Jesus story was the central theme of Western civilization.

With the Renaissance, we turned more inward—to begin examining ourselves more closely—and more outward—to begin our close inspection of nature. Hamlet, the first great modern introspective hero, was, as Freud realized, a modern Oedipus; but Freud failed to see how Hamlet is also a modern filicide who, from beginning to end, is controlled by the dead hand of his father.

Our turning outward bore successful fruit in the form of science and technology; if the modern filicidal patriarchy feels compelled to justify itself, it does so by call-ing attention to the success of its scientific and technological creations. It remained for a woman to reduce our scientific behavior to its mythic essence and in doing so reveal for all who would look the filicidal roots of "modern man." A hundred and fifty years ago we men unwittingly sat for our portrait. The picture Mary Shelley produced in *Frankenstein* is somewhat less flattering and considerably more truth-ful than the allegedly loftier works of great art produced by various of her male contemporaries.

The Frankenstein myth is central to our age and to our understanding of our-selves, not merely because of its depiction of the dangers of unbridled science. Much more, it is central because it contains the most concise representation we have of the actual, filicidal politics of the modern family and of modern society. In her main characters, Shelley sketched modern filicidal man with astonishingly detailed insight: Victor Frankenstein is compulsively self-destructive, driven by forces he cannot recognize to create a *son* by his own efforts and without the troublesome involve-ment of a woman. Having created such a son, he is horrified by the ugliness of his creation and rejects him totally, thereby turning the son into the very monster whose existence he had always denied in himself.

Two popular contemporary myths are permutations of the Frankenstein story. HAL 9000, the thinking and feeling computer in *2001: A Space Odyssey*, on whom literal filicide is committed by the astronauts, is merely a purified version of all the mythic victims of filicide before him. In *Myra Breckinridge,* finally, we shall see how the confused and introverted realities of modern filicide achieve their most surprising and poignant representation.

•

To appreciate the filicidal elements in the mythic remnants of our past, we have first to look more closely at our own behavior. One way to do this is to use the child as mirror—comparing the seemingly infinite potential of the infant with the highly restricted behavior of adults, all the while wondering how we get from one to the other by a process which we, with straight adult faces, call growth.

Literal filicide, that is, actual physical murder of infants and children, was common in the ancient world. Progress is, among other things, an increasing tendency toward behavioral filicide. By various means we force the son and the daughter into the sex-determined roles of "masculinity" and "femininity." Appropriate "masculine" behavior in the son is rewarded; inappropriate behavior is punished. Appropriate "feminine" behavior in the daughter is rewarded; inappropriate behavior is punished. The primary method of reward is acceptance of the son or daughter as a well-behaved member of filicidal society. The primary method of punishment is rejection: the son or daughter is directly or indirectly threatened with exclusion from the family and from society. Knowing that violence is not limited to physical mutilation but may just as easily be a matter of mental coercion, we begin to understand how filicide, as one of the central formative experiences of infancy and childhood, indoctrinates all sons and all daughters into a world in which violence is assumed—without anybody ever talking about it—to be the normal means by which one deals with, and gets on in, the world.

This sort of behavior may once have aided us in establishing a foothold on the planet and in surviving with a degree of security and serenity. Now such behavior has become one of the chief threats to our survival, since it is one of the chief, and most thoroughly concealed, ways in which the whole system of violent behavior is passed on from one generation to the next. We are conscious neither of the filicide committed on us nor of the filicide we are presently committing on the current generation of children. In our amnesiac ignorance we continue to plant the seeds of violence in every new generation, while consciously we carry about with us and profess the best of intentions and the most loving of attitudes toward our children.

While we have made some progress in creating a world of fuller stomachs, healthier bodies, better shelter, and more creative employment, we are still ruled by sons (this being a filicidal patriarchy) who were killed by their fathers and mothers and who, with our tacit or explicit approval, continue to conduct affairs of state in the same threatening, militaristic way as all our leaders have done throughout history.

The theory of filicide deals with a stratum of behavior which lies deep beneath that touched by ideology. Through filicide we can see why political revolutions of whatever kind inevitably degenerate into internecine violence, and why the leaders who emerge from revolutions turn out to be much the same kind of rulers as were their pre-revolutionary forebears. Nowhere in the world is love a factor in councils of state because nowhere in the world can we find leaders who have not been indoctrinated as infants and children into the system of filicidal violence as the norm of human behavior. As long as we remain unconscious of filicide, our best attempts to deal with the problem of violence will be mocked by spectacular, ever more bloody failure.

The origins of filicide are lost in that obscuring mist of pre-history which we are now only beginning to see as containing something more than grave artifacts and crude examples of architecture. It is clear that historical humanity is filicidal humanity; by the time history begins we are already filicidal through and through. Even the evidence slowly coming to light concerning the existence of a widespread matriarchy in our prehistorical past demonstrates that whether mothers or fathers are the central agents of power, filicidal behavior has been the human way for a very long time.

On the smaller scale, for the individual filicide begins at home. Adults who are parents indoctrinate, more or less unconsciously, their children in the appropriate role. This being a patriarchy, the father functions as the primary agent of filicide— the court of first and last resort. The mother plays an accessorial role. She may employ nonmasculine behavior toward the son and nonfeminine behavior toward the daughter only as long as that behavior does not conflict with the father's partly conscious and partly unconscious understanding of the two roles. In families without a father or with a father who for some reason does not play the proper filicidal role, the mother is fully equipped—being, remember, a fully indoctrinated filicide herself—to take over.

The heterosexual nuclear family remains the central model in our civilization because of a peculiar, perhaps even perverted emotional dynamic. It functions like this: filicide results in adult personalities one of whose primary traits is self-hatred. This self-hatred comes partly from the fact that, as a child, one unconsciously perceives that the parent of one's own sex—on whom one is to model oneself—is a victim of filicide and a perpetrator as well. The perception is unconscious. The resulting repressed hatred of that parent can only be transferred to oneself, since the child is a "success" precisely to the degree that it learns that parent's mode of being. Then, as an adult, one enters a world in which one is expected to make the primary emotional commitment to a person of the other sex. The entangled confusion of love-hate which one long ago felt toward one's parent of the same sex is, if one is "normal," then left unattended to for the remainder of one's life. Traditional, compulsive, heterosexual marriage is thus always undercut by this haunting, unexamined need to come to terms with the persons of one's own sex, all of whom are identified with the original perpetrator of filicide.

Here perhaps lies the origin of our taboo against homosexual behavior. Certainly the severity of the taboo is a reflection of an emotional reality which is inadmissible: namely, the unresolved hatred of one's same-sex parent. In the nuclear family the self-hatred then focuses in the next generation on the child of one's own sex, who with its child's sensitivity cannot but be aware of and learn the hatred as part of the filicidal package. The parent then finds the only permissible emotional outlet in the child of the opposite sex. The emotional dynamic of the heterosexual nuclear family winds up looking like this:

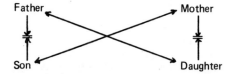

The emotional lines from Father to Son and from Mother to Daughter are blocked by the on-going reality of filicide. The desperately needed internal resolution of self-hatred is also blocked within the family. The father teaches the son to hate himself as much as the father hates himself. The mother teaches the daughter to hate herself as much as the mother hates herself. One is thus forced into the paradoxical position of seeking the path to self-love in the form of the person of the other sex—that is, in the form of the person who, according to the rigid, compartmentalized role distinctions implanted in this culture, is most unlike oneself.

This paradox, which entraps us all, is obviously irresolvable within the confines of the traditional heterosexual nuclear family. In that tiny framework it provides the emotional energy for the compulsive, unconscious continuation of the same patterns of relationship when the son and daughter grow up and have children of their own. The solution to this filicidal conundrum has nothing to do with homosexuality as such. The taboo, as noted, is significant especially because of its severity; but homosexual relationships appear to be neither more nor less prone to filicidal behavior. A solution is approached by finding and using ways of lifting oneself above the chains of the filicidal paradox, by learning physically and mentally that there is far more to oneself and to one's potential than the confining and stultifying experience of our sex-roles indicates. One learns, in other words, that I am far more than this "I," than this gender-based personality, that this "I" encompasses much more than its "masculinity" or its "femininity."

Filicidal behavior is not confined to the home, nor to childhood, nor to our behavior toward children. In the myriad power hierarchies—social, occupational, educational, religious, etc.—that make up our lives, any person with more power functions in a fatherly or motherly filicidal way toward any person with less power. In such situations the person with less power functions as son or daughter. Our daily lives are filled with replications, large and small, threatening and trivial, of our original filicidal experience. Since a given person may occupy a position of great power in one hierarchy and a position of lesser power in another, in our daily lives we are constantly interchanging roles. The whole system of filicidal values and behavior survives partly because of this constant practice of our dual skills at being fathers and mothers, sons and daughters, as the occasion demands.

The women's movement is an example of a group of people making constructive efforts to cast off the chains of compulsive, unconscious, filicidally based sex-roles. Feminist literature is, in effect, a continuing report on the nature and extent of the filicide committed on daughters. It is also a continuing report on various attempts to act above and beyond filicide. Much of the negative reaction to the women's movement becomes more comprehensible when viewed in the light of the theory of filicide. Many adult men and women are so trapped in their double roles as victims and perpetrators of filicide that they cannot conceive of any other kind of behavior except violence. They thus perceive the suggestions, analyses, demands, and changing lives that grow from and through the women's movement as violent threats to themselves. For them, every human encounter is on some level filicidal. That human beings might act from some other, nonviolent base, is for them inconceivable.

Adults who either consciously or unconsciously delight in taking their turn in murdering the next generation of sons and daughters will tend to see the theory of filicide as accusatory; it is a threat to their getting their turn at the literal or figurative paddle. Even in the face of such obtuseness, the theory of filicide is nonaccusatory, because each of us is either a murdered son or a murdered daughter. We are all victims. But we are also all perpetrators of filicide—overtly if we are parents, covertly if we are not. There is no group which we can isolate this time, whether according to their sex, their religion, or their race, on whom we can blame our filicidal guilt. We are all to blame, all equally implicated.

The theory of filicide does, as will become apparent, contain an implicit bias. It is an argument in favor of and in defense of our murdered children. The traditional terms used to discuss the problems of "child-rearing" are themselves heavily bi-

17

ased in favor of the parents and their adult society. Many adults, with their vested emotional interest in the continued functioning of a filicidal society, would treat in quite a different way the material I use in this book. They would see, as their fathers and mothers have done throughout history, filicidal behavior as beneficial and necessary. For them, child-rearing is actually a matter of child-taming. It is one thing to break a horse. It is quite another thing to break a horse's spirit.

2. FILICIDAL IMPERATIVES

The rules of filicide are unwritten, but they are more binding on us all than the terms of any written contract. They are behavioral imperatives operating at such a deep and hidden level that they may be easily mistaken for the human equivalent of animal instinct. A number of observers of the human condition, past and present, have, in fact, concluded that the behavior based on these rules is immutable (human nature), or, if mutable, then only with the greatest effort (will power, discipline, conditioning, psychosurgery, mind-altering drugs).

We take these rules and the resultant behavior so much for granted that, in a sense, we have become the rules. It is difficult for us to conceive of ourselves as men and women in any other way except in accordance with the rules of-filicidal behavior. We have constructed whole philosophies of life, of government, of science, of art, of religion, to justify and ennoble our filicidal behavior.

We may have the ability to be free and the potential to exercise free will. As long as we remain so nearly perfectly amnesiac concerning filicide, such abilities and potentials are merely so much unused, rusting machinery. In pain almost too great to bear—certainly it is too great for our infant minds to deal with directly—we at a very early age forget the two terrible facts of our earliest life: parent as murderer, and child-self as victim. And we forget we have forgotten. We then set about emulating the behavior of our inadvertently murderous parents as we construct amnesiac lives as much like their amnesiac lives as possible. "Maturity," that is, socially respectable and responsible adulthood, becomes an endless series of self-deceptive maneuvers designed to establish and affirm for oneself and one's own time the unconscious belief in filicidal existence as normal and healthy.

Out of this double amnesia grows a profound hypocrisy that haunts us all our days and follows us even—especially—into sleep. Filicide, with its concommitant amnesia, results in a splitting not just of the personality but of the very self. In fact, what we call the personality—that is, the persona, the "person" who I think myself to be, this filicidal "me"—is the behavioral entity occupying the visible, public side of that schism of the self. It is an almost robot-like creature whose choices and movements are almost wholly determined by fear. "I" am a defense mechanism, constructed in desperation out of the fear of filicide committed on me and the fear of the memory of that deed. As long as I do not recognize and act on the knowledge of the source of my fear, my desperate search for security and serenity is doomed. It is to this anesthetized, sleeping creature, this part of the larger self, that the platitudes of behaviorism speak with such forceful relevance and validity. The murdered self can only conclude that beyond freedom and dignity lies a wasteland of violent conditioning, because it has never known freedom and dignity.

Whatever it is that exists on the other side of the schism of the self, we hide it from other people and from ourselves as well. There one finds those qualities and potentials we occasionally glimpse in the works of genius and in the lives of those whom we call holy or brave or inspired—or mad.

Nietzsche spoke in disgust of "the disease called man." The symptoms may be those of disease; but the theory of filicide makes clear that the cause is a prison of our own devising. So great was our perceived guilt that we even came to believe that the sacrifice of a god was required to remove it.

The filicidal schism is very nearly perfect. The ever-increasing pain and confusion of our private and planetary lives is eloquent testimony to its near perfection. The schism is imperfect to the extent that, as we have continued to rape ourselves, our children, and the world, we have made some genuine progress in humanitarian behavior. Our private and public consciences still function, though our pain and frustration grow seemingly beyond bearing as our best-intended, most humane efforts are shattered again and again in poisonous explosions of violence.

We forget the murderous act which shapes our lives, but we continue to live—automaton-like, perhaps, but we do continue to live. In describing now the filicidal ways in which we live, I will use R.D. Laing's model of "rules." The rules of filicidal behavior are not actually rules as we usually think of the term. Perhaps something like "existential imperative" would be more accurate, for these "rules" are, in effect, behavioral commands—for the most part nonverbal—"given" to us as infants and children regarding the ways in which we must exist if we are to survive.

But even to speak of "existential imperatives," one still risks cataloging, compartmentalizing that which cannot be cataloged and compartmentalized. Our behavior is an organic, synergistic whole which cannot be so reduced without destroying the unity we are trying to understand. To avoid as much as possible the reductive distortions of a list of filicidal rules, I will speak first of the central imperative of filicidal behavior, which is *control*, and then sketch some of the principal variations on that basic "rule."

This list which is no list should in no way be taken as exhaustive. To discuss our actual, real behavior as opposed to our pretended, ideal behavior is to find boxes within boxes within boxes. The best one can hope for with words is to point here and there and say, "Let us look in this box and see what it holds, and then in the box inside that box, and then in the box inside that box inside that box." Like the regress of images between two facing mirrors, the series is infinite and, to the linear mind, disorienting. Fortunately it is not the series but the experience of the perception of the series that is important.

It is difficult to speak of our experience of filicide because, while it is universal, it is also universally forgotten. Nothing that I say here about filicide is unknown to any of us. It is just that we have all been a bit absent-minded about one of our basic, formative experiences. In the metaphor, we have forgotten both the perception of the infinite regress as well as the images themselves. In his own delving into the hidden recesses of the politics of the family, Laing discovered the existence not only of unstated "rules" but of unstated "meta-rules." Laing's meta-rules are two in number. The first states that the "rules" do not exist. The second states that neither the existence nor the nonexistence of the rules or the meta-rules is to be thought about or discussed. Here we have the source of our double amnesia. In fear we forget our filicidal experience; in greater fear we then forget we have forgotten.

CONTROL

The central rule of the behavior which grows out of filicide is: control. Because the central fact of filicide is that it is a controlling act. *Homo sapiens,* as we know it, as we are it, is the controlling animal. All other rules of filicidal behavior are implicit in the one rule: control.

Men and women center their lives around control, though in somewhat different ways. A man is successful to the extent that he directly and consciously controls himself, members of his family, his work, and his world. A man is a failure to the extent that he does not control in this way. A woman is successful to the extent that she indirectly and unconsciously controls herself, members of her family, her household—which is both her work and her world. A woman is a failure to the extent that she does not control in this way.

Confusion arises in societies in which the roles develop in such a way that one parent—in this patriarchy it has traditionally been the man—spends large amounts of time away from the home. In such cases the mother not infrequently becomes the de facto center of control.

The parent, in committing filicide on the son or daughter, is controlling the son or daughter by literally creating the child's personality in the image of the parent. Filicide is the ultimate possible behavioral control. The primary formative experience of the human being as infant is that the way one gets on in this world is by being controlled, and by controlling. Such intimate interference is only violence in the guise of parental love. The pattern of the lives of humans is thus set very early.

As infants we are controlled through some form of physical punishment, ranging from the blatant cruelty of physical pain to the less obvious physical punishment which consists of the withholding of physical affection. As we grow we find ourselves being controlled ever more abstractly by the threat of withheld parental approval of our actions. "Growing up" is a series of tests concerning how well we are learning to be filicidal human beings. As we enter adult society, other rewards—those of status, power, and money—are dangled before us to coax our obedience. Hidden behind those rewards are the threats of adult, societal filicide. The principal agents at the adult level are a primitive police force, and the principal setting is an equally primitive prison system.

Our mindless obedience as adults to the unwritten dictates of society springs from the original act of filicidal control by our parents. Our pre-verbal perception of the filicide committed on us all teaches us that our physical survival depends on massive, in fact, organismic capitulation to the demands made on us by our parents. The inequality of the filicidal confrontation—the infant is no match physically or mentally for its parents—has many later ramifications. It produces a civilization built on such peculiar equations as:

- bigger = better,
- more = better,
- faster, higher, longer, newer, etc. = better.

In our double amnesia we are constantly and desperately seeking to prove to ourselves and to the world that we are at least as "big" as those creatures who committed filicide on us so long ago. What we are actually seeking to prove is that we are as filicidal, which is to say, as successful at controlling, as they were. It is an impossible quest (as so much of our literature shows); even in our adult bodies we are still acting and reacting unconsciously, in the manner of that infant-child killed in the forgotten past. At the most basic level the self still sees itself as being *that* small, which means its deeds can never raise it to the stature of the human giants it perceived hovering over it as control was originally established. Our most important product, progress, is therefore ultimately our most frustrating experience.

The inequality of size and mental ability in the original filicidal confrontation also produces a society founded on competitiveness as the highest good. Control, if successful, means that somebody wins and somebody loses. There is no sense of shared experience. In the proto-scene there is no sense of parent and child growing together or exploring joyfully the world both inhabit. Parent wins; child loses.

22

And child spends the rest of its life trying to win, never realizing that the parent did not really win but was compulsively continuing the ancient human losing streak. One of the reasons we fear sex so much is that it is a game in which, when well played, everybody wins.

For the son, the universal lesson of filicide is: control at any cost. That is, if all other means of attempted control fail, the son is not only justified in resorting to physical control (violence), he is expected to resort to it. The filicidal end—control—justifies any means--up to and including whatever amount of violence is necessary to achieve control. We punish those who are "irrationally" violent (murderers), while we reward and revere those who are "rationally" violent (statesmen and soldiers). In our amnesia we are unaware that everybody loses in the game of violence—that the parent lost just as much as did the child in the act of filicide. We fail to see that any kind of destructive behavior is at bottom self-destructive. Following the insatiable and compulsive need to control, we get to the point where we are today: so nearly perfect has our control become that we have turned the planet itself into a delicately fused nuclear bomb.

For the daughter, the universal lesson of filicide is the same: control at any cost. But the method is different. In this patriarchy a woman's control is necessarily subtler, since her filicide teaches her that she is to be physically and intellectually weaker than the man. Her control has been based traditionally on the assigned "feminine" qualities such as emotionality, coyness, and so on. The tool of her control has been the only negotiable commodity allowed to her: her body. Thus her chief source of power is sex. As the daughter grows up she further learns that her area of control is confined to the home, specifically to the day-to-day details of "raising" the children. All other areas of life are off-limits. When the children have grown up and moved away, the woman is left to become that almost lifeless ornamental figure of devout reverence embodied in the familiar stereotype: Mother.

We have many names for control: we manage, we manipulate, we persuade, we coerce, we educate, we enlighten, we advertise, we rape, we fuck, we fight, we kill, we love, we hate, we convert, we capitalize, we ostracize, we imprison, we punish, we fine, we execute, we theorize, we attack, we legislate, we adjudicate, we research, we build, we destroy—all in mindless imitation of the frightening, intimidating, paralyzing, numbing, brutally manipulative act of filicide perpetrated on us before we could begin asking proper questions about the world.

All other filicidal imperatives grow out of our need to control. They are variations on the basic theme of control. Developed over the millennia, they are the most effective means to the end of control. In discussing now these other "rules," what we are actually looking at is the best ways to be a successful filicide. Filicide is a double-edged sword. It is the means by which the parent controls the child, and the means by which the child-as-adult controls its life and world, including its own children.

EMULATION

Given the division and distance between the two sex roles, the child tends to emulate the parent of its own sex. While the miming extends to all areas—gesture, dress, grooming, speech, permissible activities—its basic effect occurs in the way one shapes one's consciousness. Mentally, the emulation imperative comes out something like this:

> • For male children: *Be rational; do not be emotional.*
> • For female children: *Be emotional; do not be rational.*

The son learns the value of what the culture defines as intelligence as the primary means to the end of control. If the son fails as a man, it is because he was not smart enough. He was dumb. Compulsive rationality is the masculine way of filicidal knowledge. Man the thinker keeps his cool, exhibits grace under pressure, thinks before he acts—unless of course he has been trained rationally to act mindlessly, like a soldier, say.

This rule comes into occasional conflict with the control imperative, which seems to say: *Win at any cost.* Through the ages we have learned the value of cooperation as a means to the end of collective control. The amount of pain which such cooperation, especially in this corporate age with its emphasis on teamwork, has caused within masculine souls is incalculable. Every team member has been trained from infancy to aspire to one goal—to be the leader, to be in control. Nowadays we have got to the place where we measure much of our progress and much of our individual success by the extent to which various team members are able to control their desire to control. This suppression produces many of the characteristics of modern living as we know it: behavior based on dissimulation, dishonesty toward oneself and toward others, selfishness, and so on, with all those qualities highlighted by not infrequent outbursts of rage and fury. Where the anger and frustration at having to control one's control remains bottled up, it often surfaces in other self-destructive ways, such as smoking or drinking, not to mention the various hypertensive maladies.

For the son the obverse of the rationality rule is: *do not be emotional.* Which is to say: *freeze.* Deny your emotions, your ability to give affection along with your need to receive affection. As the father murders the son by rejecting him as an independent entity and by forcing him into the masculine mold, the son also murders himself by restricting his method of experiencing and dealing with himself and the

24

world to the ways of rational control. The emotional freeze of masculinity is the specific means by which one isolates oneself from everything in the universe outside one's own rational, controlling consciousness. It is the means by which we create lives and societies characterized by alienation—from self, from other people, from nature. Without the empathy which a growing and healthy emotionality imparts, every person and every object becomes a distant *thing* to be used, manipulated, and controlled. The masculine ego in its emotional isolation and paralysis can assume only that it is king of all it surveys and then act to the fullest on that assumption.

The son compares the way his father behaves toward him physically with the way his mother behaves toward him physically. The father touches very little. The mother touches a great deal. What conclusion can the son draw but that the father's far greater physical distance indicates that the father perceives the son's body as ugly and unlovable? This early impression is confirmed many times over as the son grows and observes how the father deals with his own body and with the bodies of other men, and learns how fathers in the past have dealt with the bodies of other men. The physical distance between father and son combines with the gradual death of the son's emotionality to produce a masculine attitude toward one's body which might best be described—so intense is it—as one of malignant indifference. Only a creature which hates its own body can do, or allow to be done, to other bodies those bloody things men have done and continue to do to each other and to women and children.

Not infrequently as one achieves some level of security, masculine alienation becomes so severe that the lives of men are partially directed toward finding ways to overcome the alienation. Our many such attempts, even the cleverest of them, have failed because we have relied on the very behavior which produced the alienation in the first place, that of compulsively rational control. Masculine visions of the end of history tend to be empty. Marx saw literally nothing at the point where the dialectic of history would have at last moved us beyond communism. The word "utopia" is based on Greek roots meaning "nowhere." Whatever Jesus' vision of heaven may have been, we have turned it into a realm of existence in which all but the most vegetable of us would be bored silly. Orthodox masculine rationality is incapable of contemplating or conceiving of the validity of any mode of experience other than its own.

For the daughter the central meaning of the emulation imperative is: *be emotional.* In practice the result is what has been traditionally thought of as typically feminine behavior, ranging from the social mannerism known as "flightiness" to the heavier burden of compulsive emotionality known as "love." The daughter, having at least on the surface abdicated responsibility for her rational and intellectual abilities, becomes the universal source of emotional support and compassion. Daughter-as-woman is supposed to forgive men everything, including our most repulsive and repetitive acts of violence on the bodies of women.

Since women cannot think, they are supposed to feel. They are of course not allowed to participate in rational discussions of a crisis, whether these discussions take the form of the man's problems at work or the form of global councils of war.

Just as the father's physical distance from the son reinforces a behavior in the son centered on hatred, the mother's physical closeness to the daughter reinforces a behavior centered on love. As the rational qualities of her mind are repressed, the daughter pays more attention to her emotionality and to her body as a tool, a means of expressing herself and her emotions. Women have been fully as involved and implicated as have men in the long process by which they have been turned into sex objects.

Each filicide, whether on the son or the daughter, results in behavior so exaggerated that we would surely long ago have died laughing at ourselves if we did not consider the behavior so normal. Masculine behavior is a tragicomic acting out of a very peculiar misapprehension of the nature of genuine rationality. Feminine behavior is a tragicomic acting out of a very peculiar misapprehension of the nature of genuine emotionality. One is tempted to describe the two behaviors as childish. In the terms of filicidal reality they *are* childish. When we filicides say "childish," we mean something less than human, something mindless, verging on the idiotic. The father freezes the son into a rigid mold of emotionless rational control. The mother smothers the daughter into a rigid mold of nonrational emotional control disguised as weakness and dependence. It is all "childish"—but only as long as we accept the old view of children as nothing more than filicidal adults-in-the-making.

That rationality of which we speak here is at best a pseudorationality. Filicidal man is so thoroughly indoctrinated into compulsive rationality that he rarely glimpses any possibility that men may also be something other than rational and that that something might be as good as being rational. The son's rationality becomes compulsive and all-consuming. He can't stop thinking. The successful man is a thinking machine, always cool, always planning, always scheming, contriving, coping rationally. We accept this kind of rationality because it promises great things—successful control and thus security—and because it frequently seems to deliver on that promise.

The fact that it is a pseudorationality may be seen in two ways—first, in the ever more apparent and dangerous flaws in this civilized world our rationality has created; and second, in the lives of individual men who fail, who do not win in the way men are supposed to win.

The lower and middle echelons of all occupational hierarchies are filled with the tragic figures of men who, having failed in the rational way of knowledge as it applies to their lives, are left with little to do but live out their days in a kind of zombie-like trance. On the more grandiose level one sees a similar kind of existential shock in petty tyrants who have fallen off their thrones. Our so-called rationality offers us almost no preparation for anything except the success which presumably comes from exercise of that rationality. One would think it obvious that a genuinely rational approach to life would include attention to one's growth in areas other than that of compulsive rationality—such as those in which one for a time would stop being rational. Obvious examples are those areas of experience concerning emotional and spiritual growth, yet they are so unknown to men as to be alien and frightening. Our excessive and irrational fear as a society of mind-altering drugs surely stems from an awareness that our much-vaunted rationality is actually a very weak and fragile thing.

The traditional rationality of men is of course not rationality at all but an unthinking, compulsive imitation of the father's consciousness, which itself was but an unthinking imitation of his father's consciousness, and so on in infinite regression beyond the beginnings of history.

A similar analysis applies to the emotionality of women. Men think of women as weak because they are so emotional. Many women think of themselves as weak for the same reason. Genuine noncompulsive emotionality with its ready laughter and ready compassion is as rare in women as genuine noncompulsive rationality with its symbol-manipulative virtuosity and its joyous games-playing is in men. Yet the potential for such emotionality is just as surely one of our greatest potential sources of health in dealing with the vicissitudes of this life.

Emulative confusions abound, a fact which only adds to our difficulties as children in constructing proper filicidal personalities. For a given son, his mother's emotionality may be much more convincing as a way of dealing with the world than is his father's poorly developed rationality. Or for a daughter, her father's rationality may be far more attractive than her mother's flighty emotionality. We all of course learn our filicidal lessons from both parents as well as from the society at large. Our individual perception and practice of the combinations and nuances of the various imperatives result in a wide range of private and public behavior which, in practice, often has little direct relation to the sex of a given individual. But all the while we maintain the rigid public pretense that: *Dad is a real man, Mom is a real woman, and, depending on whether I have a penis or a vagina, I'm doing my best to be one or the other.*

27

CAUTION

The principal motivation behind our filicidal behavior is fear. As infants we can perceive the fact that we survive our violent indoctrination into the beginning stages of adulthood only in negative terms. So overwhelming and painful is the enforced adjustment and narrowing of our consciousness by parents and society that we must conclude that the filicidal agents stop short of our physical death not out of love but for reasons as obscure as the reasons for filicide itself. The whole process is so painful and mysterious, and our resultant belief in our own value and integrity so precarious, that our lives from then on are characterized by the exercise of extreme caution. Another of the imperatives is: *be careful—all the time.*

A man is successful to the extent that, as he seeks rational and emulative control, he does not make mistakes. Spontaneity is to be avoided because it is behavior in which control is relinquished. Sex is such a problem for us in part because full sexual release means that for a time one has to give up rational control of oneself. The son learns that spontaneity involving other people is advisable only in circumstances where the behavioral limits are clearly defined. Note, for example, that business law is the only area of legal activity in which all fifty states have adopted the same code. The son learns he may be somewhat more spontaneous in his exploration and exploitation of the world of things (science and technology), because, if you are just a little careful, objects will usually not hit back the way people will.

A woman's caution centers initially around her body and her sex. As her sole area of control, her body must be kept ready for her husband. There is a second, terrible area of control which females learn. It concerns the ways in which the woman may fall victim to masculine violence. While the woman may have great sexual power, she must exercise it very carefully. If pushed too far, the man may lose control. In such a case, the nearest woman is likely to be the immediate object of masculine fury in the form of rape or murder—this apart from the fact that such attacks may occur without warning and with no provocation on the part of the woman.

Masculine pride is such in this patriarchy that the man can see no limits to the areas of his life where he must exercise caution. Everything is his responsibility (or so he thinks)—at home, at work, internally, externally. The caution of the woman-as-mother is centered in her home and her children. Restricted to that tiny world, the mother is frequently driven to the most extreme forms of possessiveness as a means of fearfully cautious control.

For both men and women, the caution rule effectively teaches: *Don't trust anyone or anything, including yourself.* Without trust, relaxation—mental or physical—is impossible. Which means we come to exist in an uninterrupted state of mental and physical tension. And being unable to trust further means we are unable to love.

In the confusing maze of our lives based on these hidden imperatives, the only people we can love are people who have agreed to participate in, or who have already participated in, an intimate filicidal event or relationship with us: our parents, our spouses, and our children. In this reality, "I love you" too often means, "I like to be filicidal with you"—for filicidal behavior is the only historically successful interactive model we have.

DISSIMULATION

The brutal experience of filicide at the hands of the persons on whom one is completely dependent and whom one is supposed to honor, if not love, causes even the best of our later behavior to be based on a foundation of deceit and dissimulation. As long as the realities of our behavior are not faced they must produce a deep-seated hatred toward the perpetrators of filicide. But such hatred is inadmissible in the social reality each generation inherits. So we must pretend love and deny hatred toward the persons who have in effect murdered us. Any real love or gratitude we may feel toward our parents is rather thoroughly poisoned by, first, the unresolved and very powerful negative emotions we feel toward them, and second, by our pretension that those emotions do not exist. Our genuine, deep feelings of love are smothered under a blanket of social and familial duplicity.

The dissimulation toward one's parents as individuals fits into a larger pattern of social deceit. As children we are continuously indoctrinated verbally into a set of attitudes labeled "goodness" and "proper behavior," which is superficially at variance with the deeper, on-going filicidal indoctrination. On the surface the parental lesson is simple: *Do as I say.* Observing the inconsistencies in adult behavior, children rapidly realize that there is an unstated clause here: *Do as I say and not as I do.* The real parental lesson—the one which produces the actual behavior desired—is a bit more complex: *do as I do even though it seems like I am teaching you to do as I say and not as I do.* In other words: *dissimulate.*

It is this early, basic lesson in dissimulation which produces the later widespread behavior in which, for example, a person when challenged for alleged wrong-doing convincingly denies any error whatsoever. Filicidally that person is correct: the person was only doing what was perceived as correct. Persons whom we call criminals frequently assert their innocence even when confronted with the most conclusive evidence to the contrary. Their problem is: they did not learn the intricate ways in which one is permitted and expected to be dishonest. Not having learned this lesson, they are failures, filicidally. It is that failure—and not the overstepping of certain moral or legal boundaries which makes them criminal in the eyes of society. As unsuccessful filicides they cannot see the justice of filicidal injustice.

Functioning on the basis of this imperative to dissimulate, our virtuous behavior remains virtuous only as long as it produces the desired effect: control and survival at any cost. Hence the ease with which we, as societies and as individuals, resort to physical violence as an ultimate solution. Through our deep-seated dissimulation we learn the efficacy of pretended trust and pretended virtue. When a crisis occurs, when a breach of this shallow trust happens, or when an assault is made on our fragile virtue, it is only human nature—as we all know—to respond in ways which totally give the lie to our supposed trust and virtue. Our unfaced, unexpressed anger at our own dissimulation warps our sense of equitable justice. We want not merely an eye for an eye, but two—or ten—eyes for each one lost.

The parent sells its own dissimulation to the child as part of the larger package of filicidal behavior. We never say these things, not with words, but our behavior communicates them constantly. If one could reduce the sales pitch to words, it might sound something like this:

> *If you ever doubt the value of dissimulation, just remember this. Would I, your parent, your creator, who loves you and to whom you are the most important person in the world—as you can tell by the many sacrifices I have to make to put up with and train such an unworthy creature as yourself—would I have done what I have done to you if I, who am so much older, wiser, bigger, and stronger, were not absolutely convinced that it is for the best? My behavior toward you may seem at times rough, brutal, even cruel. It seems so precisely because you are only a child, while I am an adult and furthermore an adult who is your parent and who therefore loves you and whom you therefore must love. It is because I love you that I do these things to you which hurt me as much as they hurt you—but for which you will one day thank me.*

And sure enough, assuming that we learn and follow the rules, that day arrives when we, as successful grown-ups, do thank them. By definition, the successful grown-up is the person who successfully forgets the filicidal experience and who also forgets the act of forgetting. Obviously, the successful grown-up child can never be grateful enough because—again, by definition—to be successful, the grown-up child must be convinced of its own ugliness, its own unworthiness. As a proper grown-up it can only marvel at its parents for having done so much for such an unlovable creature.

For the man the dissimulation rule effectively states:

> *You are what you do, because what you are is nothing.*

Hence the masculine drive for accomplishment, for successful control of the world.

Hence the ease with which the man comes to build his identity around his job, his work. Hence the masculine emphasis on the importance of reputation. What other people, outside authorities, judge a man to be is all that matters. Reputation allows us to move somewhat more easily into the dreaded experience of old age with its alleged frightening loss of control and then to accept the far more dreaded experience of the ultimate loss of control, death, with a certain forced equanimity. We know our survivors will treasure our memory: *He was a good man.*

For the woman the dissimulation rule effectively states:

> *You are what you are, and nothing you do can change that fact.*

In this patriarchy what she is, of course, is "woman"—not a female human being with all the potential that implies, but "woman": the person restricted to the narrowly defined role of reproductive and child-rearing machine prescribed by generations of mothers and fathers. To the extent that the daughter successfully deceives herself and other people concerning her actual human potential, she concentrates on what she is taught to perceive as her "self," that is to say, on her body. Beauty becomes the chief criterion by which daughters judge themselves and by which sons judge daughters. As the daughter ages, her homemaking abilities take on additional significance. The ability to make a good apple pie or to iron a good shirt may override shortcomings in physical appearance.

Both men and women come to judge themselves by externals. We then deny our inherent worth. One of the great filicidal virtues resulting from this denial is a very peculiar kind of selflessness. We find ourselves living our lives for other people, primarily our spouses and our children. Fathers in this patriarchy are able to justify almost any destructive behavior they may wish to undertake by thinking: *I'm doing this for my family.* "This" may be anything from working eighteen hours a day to making a wasteland of some small foreign country. The mother can justify her own destructive behavior, which in this patriarchy is almost wholly self-directed, in the same way: *It is worth it to smother myself and my talents here in this house because I am doing it for my family.* So perfectly, if distortedly, selfless has this living for one's spouse and children become that we frequently arrive at the end of our lives only to find that we have not lived at all.

NEGATIVITY

The last imperative is not so much a single command as a set of attitudes determined by the preceding imperatives. If these attitudes can be summarized in one final rule, it might be: *be negative.* With filicide as our central, personality-forming experience, we are forced to conclude that this world and this life combine to form

31

an extremely negative reality characterized by pain, suffering, and evil. These attitudes, which—like our memory of filicide—are for the most part hidden, form the actual operative attitudes by which we lead our lives and make our day-to-day, year-to-year decisions about our lives. Such a thorough-going, hidden negativity goes a long way toward undercutting even our best conscious efforts to be less controlling, less violent, less compulsively cautious. They do so by causing us to tend to see our reformative efforts in negative terms instead of in positive ones. We try to control our desire to control instead of seeking ways of being in which "control" is a noncategory.

Following is a short list of a few of the widely held, comfortable negative beliefs generated by filicide:

> It is a jungle world.
> Might makes right.
> You will lose because you don't deserve to win.
> Punishment is the only way to learn.
> It is our lot to suffer.
> Death is better than life.
> Sickness is better than health.
> Total freedom is extremely dangerous.
> Security is more precious than gold.
> You pay for what you do.
> You get what you pay for.
> Everybody is guilty but I'm guiltier than anybody.
> Everybody is afraid but I'm more afraid than anybody.
> Work is the only cure-all.
> All cures are temporary.
> It's all hopeless in the end.
> Things are what they seem to my normal, filicidal consciousness.
> Nobody, least of all me, can heal me.
> War is inevitable.
> Human nature does not change.
> Humanity is evil.
> Children are wild creatures who have to be tamed.
> Old age and senility are bad.
> Youth is foolish.
> Wisdom comes only with age.
> Our bodies are dirty.
> Our minds are dirty.

•

On the surface our implementation of these rules of filicidal behavior may seem inconsistent, possibly less than universal. As moderns, few of us are guilty of literal filicide. And few of us lead such totally desolate lives that they are not occasionally interrupted by periods of release, surcease, and rest, such as the state known as "being in love," or in the period immediately following what is called "religious conversion." That our filicide is a continuing process is indicated by the fact that such periods are brief in duration and generally weak in effect. It is not long before we fall back into our old ways.

Further, it is only in times of grave danger that our filicidal behavior becomes most apparent. The readiness with which we as nations have throughout history acceded to the periodic use of the "solution" known as war is an indication of how widespread filicidal behavior is. We know no other way as individuals. Therefore we know no other way as societies. How willingly fathers and mothers ship their sons off to those wars, and with what enthusiasm the sons allow themselves to be shipped off.

The complacency and condescension with which we view the bloody violence in the world as we sit in the serene isolation of our homes and offices is at best shortsighted and amnesiac, and at worst, dangerously self-righteous. The theory of filicide reveals the way in which we are all implicated in and by the planet-wide system of violence whether ours is the hand that wields the knife or pushes the nuclear button, or whether the hand is that of a surrogate. Our complacency is even greater in the face of the modern plague of non-bloody violence. Behavioral manipulation through various forms of subtle and overt coercion is an ancient art. The tools of science and technology have enabled us to raise that art to unprecedented levels of sophistication and to apply it to unprecedented numbers of people. In the West, we were righteously indignant, even shocked, by the phenomenon of Communist brainwashing. Such a reaction is justifiable only if we are also aware of the mind-destroying conditions in our own prisons and mental hospitals—not to mention the irony of our laissez-faire attitude toward the almost inescapable mind-rape of modern advertising.

Control, caution, rationality, emotionality—such behaviors are not in themselves destructive. It is only our compulsive and unconscious reliance on those behaviors that leads to the incessant pain and suffering of our lives. Becoming aware of one's own filicide does not mean that one then discards everything associated with filicidal behavior. It means only that one begins exploring possible solutions to the problems and challenges of existence other than those of violence.

As infants we were terrified and intimidated by the incessantly controlling behavior of our parents. In that state of terror we learned, through observation of what was being done to us and how we responded, the efficacy of violence. It worked.

We submitted. We are thus cowards from the start and (men particularly) must deny that we are by constantly proving our bravery through public displays of our ability to control. As creatures malformed through violence we seek to deny that fact in every possible way, even by crucifying those who attempt to preach and live lives of love and peace. By destroying such persons we think we have thereby won. In our amnesiac state we remain unaware of the internal price each of us pays for the false victories which violence yields. We, who are so anciently and thoroughly pervaded by violence and who cannot remember ever having been anything other than violent, are enormously threatened by anyone who will not hit back. Only the person who is not afraid can choose not to hit back. Perhaps our greatest filicidal fear is the fear of not being afraid.

Women, though their role has usually made them the bystanders as men have perpetrated the most overt and destructive physical violence, can escape their accessorial complicity only by becoming aware of their own behavioral violence. Women have great cause to hate men for having been the enforcers of the system of male-supremacy and female slavery. To respond with hatred is to respond in the values of that system. Such a response only perpetuates the whole system of violence.

A man waking up to what he has been raised to be and do with the same system has as much reason to hate other men—and women as well, for his mother after all stood to one side and allowed the filicide to happen. The filicidal trap consists in inducing us to respond over and over in kind. Hate feeds on hate. The filicidal maw of hate can never be glutted, no matter how much we feed it. It can be starved. War is only furthered by those who hate war—whether the war is between nations or within oneself. Peace comes only to those who love peace.

•

It is easy to determine whether and how well one is following the rules of filicidal behavior. If you are a man and are following the rules, other people will respect you, call you a good man, a good provider, a hard worker, a pillar of the community, pay you more money, give you more power over people and things, obey you unquestioningly, seek your advice and opinions, use you as a model for their children, and speak well of you when you are dead. If you are not following the rules, other people will laugh at you, call you a coward, sissie, queer, lazy, a poor father, pay you little money, give you little power or deprive you of whatever power you have, ignore you, get angry at you, imprison you, execute you, deride your opinions, warn their children against you, and avoid speaking of you when you are dead. If you are a woman and are following the rules, other people will call you a good wife and mother. If you are not following the rules, other people will call you a bad wife and mother, whore, bitch, shrew, dyke, man-hater, or emasculator.

Following the rules also produces a certain semantic flip-flop in one's life, hinted at in the negativity rule. What one calls pleasure becomes a kind of forced, habitual pain. What one calls love becomes a habitual action of repressing hate. Life itself is lived in a day-to-day comatose state which is usually nearer to lifelessness than to life. Death is perceived as some kind of future life in which one will somehow be rewarded for having worked so hard at not living in this life. Play becomes work, and work becomes drudgery. When one says, *I'm relaxed,* one means either, *I'm not quite as tense as I was,* or, *The aspirin/alcohol/dope/tranquilizer is working.* Sleep becomes intermittent wakefulness, and one's waking life becomes a kind of semi-articulate somnambulism.

Semantic confusions are only the surface symptoms of much deeper behavioral confusions. Where universal amnesiac behavior has existed for generations, it becomes extremely difficult to discern behavior for what it is, as opposed to what it appears to be to our well-trained, forgetful selves. Laing speaks of such convoluted behavioral inversions as knots. One such filicidal knot concerns our confused and contradictory attitude toward pleasure. The knot goes something like this:

> *Since as a result of filicide I, as a man, am not allowed to know real pleasure, I will not allow others to know pleasure, except in the behaviors which I have tested myself and know to be falsely pleasurable— though of course I pretend they are highly pleasurable. If it is necessary to allow some apparently real pleasure in others—for example, in women and children—I will view their behavior and them as vain and silly, effeminate and childish.*

In other words, private inhibitory behavior becomes public prohibitory behavior. Filicidal morals are the opiate of us all.

Another similar knot:

> *Since I, as a man, was not allowed to be weak, I will not allow others to be weak. If it is necessary to allow some weakness in others—for example, in women and children, I will deride it and despise them for their weakness.*

Or:

> *Since I, as a woman, was not allowed to be rational and intellectual, I will not allow other women to be rational and intellectual. If it is necessary to allow some rationality and intellectuality in other women, I will deride them as being masculine and butch.*

Filicide is the sins of the fathers and mothers visited on everybody unto the nth generation:

> *My parents said through their behavior that I can best control myself the way they controlled themselves. Their parents had said to them that they could best control themselves the way my grandparents controlled themselves. And so on backwards into the mists of prehistory. Therefore I am controlling myself the way my great-great-great-great-great-great grandparents told my great-great-great-great-great grandparents to control themselves. In essence I am attempting and pretending to be the same person all my forebears attempted and pretended to be.*

The rules allow so little behavioral variation that, when followed well, they produce persons who are individuals in name only. Hence our fascination with regimented schools, regimented work, football teams, and armies.

The filicidal catch is: who is that person we are all pretending to be? *It is the father/mother who never existed.* We are sons and daughters striving to be the perfectly controlling father and mother who never existed. Adulthood as we know and attempt to realize it is an illusion. The father role is an illusion. The mother role is an illusion. No wonder Kafka found an empty castle. *My guilt as a filicidal child approaches sufficiency as I approach full awareness of how   inadequately I am being my parents.* No wonder Kafka endured a trial in which no evidence against him was presented but which produced a guilty verdict and a death sentence.

> *The more inadequate I feel, the more control I exert to compensate for my feeling of inadequacy, and the more inadequate I then feel as that greater control fails to produce the desired result of making me more like my parents. So I exert still more control and feel even greater inadequacy, etc.*

Neither a man's nor a woman's work is ever done.

The behavioral variations which result from all this constitute the round-dance known as history. Since our filicidal personalities are formed by an outside agent, most of us spend our lives looking for—and often finding—some outside agent in whom we can put our trust as mindlessly as we did as infants. The agent may take the form of a person—usually the spouse, but often one's own child plays this role—or it may be an institution—a government, a nation, a religion. Filicide, since it deprives us of the opportunity to creatively participate in the free exploration of our individual potential and the formation of our personalities, forces us to the conclusion that:

> *1. The problem is me, but—*
> *2. The solution is outside of me.*

Finally, beneath all the external destructiveness which characterizes our private and public lives, is the most destructive behavior of all: the hatred of self. We never forgive ourselves for having allowed filicide to be committed on us. However irrational that attitude is—we as infants after all have little choice about what is done to us—it is the gnawing pain at the heart of our masculine and feminine souls. Self-hatred is the wellspring of human violence.

> *If I love myself, hate is impossible. If I hate myself, love is impossible. As long as I remain asleep and unaware of the filicidal processes working inside me and in the people and the world around me, I can never finally forgive the world for being so obstinately threatening, my wife for being so damnably feminine, my husband for being so damnably masculine, and my children for being so damnably childish. I cannot, because I do not know that I need to first forgive myself for letting my father and mother so limit my ability to explore and develop my potentials that they in effect killed me.*

We spend our lives running from ourselves, seeking vengeance or salvation through outside agents. In this patriarchal civilization children function universally as victims to the masculine bias of social life and the feminine bias of family life. We are buried roses in the barren garden of filicidal history.

II. THE FILICIDAL PAST

The origins of filicidal behavior are lost in the darkness of prehistory. By the time history begins, we see everywhere filicidal, patriarchal societies in which the masculine and feminine roles we know so well today are already being handed on from generation to generation. As is the case with many fundamental social phenomena, the reasons remain elusive. The fact that we are a bisexual species obviously played a role. We must have early learned the survival value and efficiency of a division of labor based on biological sex differences. Other factors—geographic, climatic, cultural—can only be guessed at.

It is possible we are dealing here with not only individual amnesia but racial amnesia as well. If a global matriarchy existed in prehistory, this patriarchal world may be the result of a violent and bloody overthrow of that matriarchy, perhaps carried out by males who were once as oppressed as females are today. Hidden in our past may be a real and vast filicide—what more brutally effective way to take vengeance on and control from the Mothers than to slaughter the children en masse? Perhaps the many myths of literal filicide from around the planet are the only way we could afford to remember such a terrible event.

Whatever lies behind it, the historical record reveals two tendencies:

- A more and more refined attempt to justify our filicidal behavior;
- A gradual intensification of that behavior.

Although our own lives bear witness to those tendencies, their general development may be seen most clearly in the major myths of the historical past. "Myth" here implies not fiction, or unreality, but precisely the opposite. The figures we encounter in myth are realer than real, larger than life, if you will. They, and the stories in which they occur, reveal in a concentrated form truths about ourselves which we easily and continuously overlook in our everyday life. Immersion in myth tempts one often to the conclusion that much of what we call life is a sort of patchwork bulwark erected over thousands of years to protect us from certain facts about ourselves and our origins we are not yet ready to face openly.

Nor does "myth" imply disbelief in the historical reality of the figures involved, particularly those of religious myth. Myth might be best understood as the consensual reality we have settled on concerning the meaning of those figures.

Two of the primary sources of myth in the Western world are Greek civilization

41

and the Judeo-Christian tradition. An examination of a few of the best-known myths from those sources will provide abundant material for understanding the emotional depth and the cultural antiquity of filicidal behavior. Perhaps even more disquieting is the ease with which one is then able to trace our filicidal myth-making up to the present day.

OEDIPUS AND JOCASTA

The myth of Oedipus tells us that the first experience which he has, soon after birth, is the proto-scene in its most basic and dangerous form. His parents attempt to kill him. His father, Laius, had been warned by the Delphic oracle that he would die at the hands of his son. When Jocasta bears him a male heir, Laius has the child exposed.

A filicidal reading of the story illuminates a number of points concerning the nature of our actual, as opposed to our pretended, behavior toward children. Of course, nowadays the story comes to us filtered through Freud. In looking again at Freud's reading of the myth, what strikes one now is the fact that he failed to find any great significance in this violent and dangerous experience to which Oedipus' parents subjected him at the beginning of his life. The fact that we have so readily gone along with the Freudian interpretation of the myth, with its profound indictment of the infant instead of the parents, says as much about our own hidden biases as about those of Freud.

Implicit in Freud's failure to see any significance in the attempted filicide at the beginning of Oedipus' life is the commonly held assumption that an infant, especially a newborn, is hardly a person at all. We view infants more as creatures with human potential who perceive what is done to them and what happens around them in only very limited ways.

With Oedipus, what is done to him is not simple filicide. Before exposing him, Laius has the infant's feet bound. Even after Oedipus is saved, he is permanently crippled as a result of the binding. ("Oedipus" = "club-foot"). In Oedipus' lameness we have an extraordinary, explicit externalization of the internal distortions caused by filicide. In this poignant sense, we are all—male and female—Oedipus.

The terrible events at the beginning of Oedipus' life form a clear micromodel of the hidden relationship between all parents and all children. As the mother to some extent actively participates but mostly gives only her passive assent, the father—in this patriarchy—forces the child into the proper behavior. Though he may not kill the child outright, he is quite likely to threaten to do so *(I'll whip you within an inch of your life)*. The parents demonstrate their power by symbolic

43

mutilation of the child (if male and American, the child has approximately a one per cent chance of avoiding circumcision). The child is then put in such a position of extreme dependence that if it survives at all, it does so on the parents' terms: as an outcast from the larger universe and as a cripple, having no conscious remembrance of the awful deed which was done to it and which makes the child into the peculiarly warped adult which it becomes.

Lame, and with a forgotten heritage of brutal violence, Oedipus survives and grows up in a foreign land. As an adult he is one day wandering about the landscape solving problems by violence (as men are wont to do). He encounters a problem in the form of a group of people blocking his path. Solution: he fights and kills one of them. His path is no longer blocked. Not realizing that his victim was in fact his father, he wanders on, arriving in Thebes where, again without knowing what he is actually doing, he eventually marries his widowed mother.

From these two deeds (killing the father, marrying the mother), Freud spun the web of Oedipal guilt in which to trap us all—male, female, father, mother, son, daughter. (Freud developed the Electra Complex, it seems, almost as an afterthought to account for the daughter's murderous jealousy of the mother.) Freud's argument is that it doesn't matter whether Oedipus knew what he was doing or not. The point was that in the family as Freud knew it and as we know it the son is doomed to feel murderous jealousy toward his father and the daughter is doomed to feel murderous jealousy toward her mother.

If we consider Freud's motives in terms of the theory of filicide, we must conclude that he was to a large extent only creating yet another version of the same self-serving adult propaganda that one finds in so many of our earliest myths. The common threat described in those myths is that of the son toward the father. Freud perceived the central meaning of the Oedipus story in the following manner. The son understands that the mother has betrayed his affection for her in the arms of the father. The son's life is therefore shaped, perhaps warped, by the repressed desire to fuck his mother and to kill his father.

Obviously both these taboos are being given expression in the Oedipus story. But if the theory of filicide is correct, what we have in this myth and in countless other early myths in which the father destroys his infant son is a very crude attempt at a plea of self-defense: *I killed my son, because if I hadn't killed him, he would have killed me.* The theory of filicide stands this defense on its head by showing that if one wishes to speak of a guilty party, it is always the father who kills the son. To interpret the *patricidal* myths as central to our culture—as Freud did—one has either to ignore or grossly misinterpret such blatantly *filicidal* stories as that of Oedipus.

The quantity of filicidal myth is, when one finally lays down the blinders which Freud placed on us all, astonishing. It is as if we could not restrain ourselves from telling the true filicidal story over and over, while realizing that we at the same time had to offer some justification for our behavior. What better way is there than to find dangerous evidence of one's own repressed, adult violence in the most helpless and defenseless of humans, in the infant, who after all cannot even speak in its own defense? The parent, unable to trust himself and knowing on some level that he does harbor violent, even murderous, tendencies, can only assume that the same is true of his children. The parent then acts toward the children is if that is the case. It then becomes the case. Filicidal behavior is a vicious circle, a feedback loop of the most exquisite perfection enclosing all humanity.

What are we to make of Oedipal guilt? is there sufficient motivation in Freud's analysis, self-serving though it is, to account for the fact that when the truth at last becomes known Oedipus' self-hatred is so great that he blinds himself? And what of Laius' and Jocasta's willingness to destroy their infant son—how does that fit in Freud's interpretation? It seems that something is missing from the Freudian reading both of the myth and of the hidden politics of the family. We could accept Freud's version of the Oedipus Complex as adequate and sufficient only if that complex does exist to some degree in us all, and *if that complex conceals behavior even more bizarre and threatening to our personalities than the killing of one's father and the marrying of one's mother.*

What the Oedipus Complex conceals is filicide. Like Oedipus, we do not remember that our mothers and fathers killed us. Also like Oedipus, we will do almost anything to avoid facing that reality, even to the point of blinding ourselves to it. For is that not what Oedipus is doing at the end of Sophocles' play? He knows then that his parents tried to kill him; yet his great lines concern only what *he* did to *them.* And he is aware that he acted in total unconsciousness, while they, when they attempted to kill him, were fully aware of what they were doing.

Every day of our fear-filled, compulsively controlled, cautious, dissimulating lives bears witness to some terrible deed hidden in our individual pasts. No matter how successful we become, how rich, how famous, how brave, how loving, how holy, how creative, there is always that gnawing terror that we cannot stop and face. So extreme is our evasive behavior that we must believe that to face it would destroy us. What actually happens is that, in order to avoid facing that terror, we construct lives and civilizations which turn out to be alarmingly self-destructive anyhow.

To recognize what was done to us means to recognize that even as adults we are fragile, delicate creatures. But a central part of cultural filicide is the presumed killing off of the weak and fragile sides of ourselves. Even women, trapped in the deceptive softness of the traditional emotional role, are at bottom filicidally as tough as men. Otherwise how could they have stomached all the blood we men have shed in the name of humanity? Male and female, we cannot forgive ourselves for what we were subjected to as children. We cannot forgive our fathers in this patriarchy for being the chief, overt, controlling agents of filicide. We cannot forgive our mothers their complicity.

The Oedipal cry is: *Mother, how could you let him do that to you?* Meaning: *How could you let him fuck you; how could you love him more than me?* Freud, with his patriarchal reading of the story and of the politics of the family, can see only the son's jealousy of the father with its resultant, repressed hatred. The relationship between the two males is seen in entirely negative terms. It is not the son's lack of love which generates Oedipal guilt. It is rather the presence of hatred and competition. To find sense in Freud's interpretation we have to believe that it is the younger and weaker of the two, the infant son, who brings this hatred and sense of violent competition into the relationship.

In Freud's world the two males can relate to each other only through competition for the female. That may be a perversely flattering situation for the female. What it implies for males is that we have no choice but to spend our lives fighting, or sublimating our desire to fight. With the Electra Complex Freud applied much the same analysis to women, who are doomed to compete with each other for the male.

The filicidal cry is: *Father and Mother, how can you both do this to me?* The betrayal is by both parents, acting in concert. Again we see how things are topsy-turvy in the myth. Oedipus' parents knew what they were doing, but in the case of cultural filicide, the parents not only are ignorant of what they are doing, they believe they are giving the child nothing but love. Here Freud encountered a problem. He could find love in the Oedipal situation only between the child and the parent of the opposite sex. Between the child and the parent of the same sex he found at best a strange, inhuman nothingness and at worst a dangerous, violent hatred.

The theory of filicide enables us to perceive the existence of some approximation of love on the part of the child and *both* parents. Freud's one-sided reading of the Oedipus story assumes that men cannot love each other and that women cannot love each other, that apparently being "human nature." Such an assumption, based as it is on adult interaction with a newborn, implies a degree of genital, sexual, and emotional identity on the part of the infant which the Oedipus Complex, if it is to stand, necessarily denies.

Freud introduced the term, "primal scene," as part of his analysis of the Oedipus story. The primal scene consists of the child's viewing of his parents having intercourse. From that sight the child supposedly concludes that his mother has betrayed him. The brutality of intercourse, as the child perceives it, is supposed to confirm the child's worst fears about his father. Here too we have another instance of self-serving patriarchal propaganda. Freud's primal scene implies a virility on the part of modern fathers and a sexually judgmental ability on the part of infants which is no more convincing than certain other of Freud's conclusions (such as those concerning female orgasm and penis envy).

What is the source of the self-destructive energy which causes Oedipus to blind himself? The theory of filicide indicates that it is that compulsive, unconscious, unexamined desire to be that perfect parent which no one has ever been. Oedipus has lived his life in an exemplary fashion, following the stated rules of his society to the best of his ability, only to find that his best-intentioned, most constructive efforts have in reality been exceedingly destructive. *The Oedipal male is characterized by a life of tragic failure.* In classical tragedy we attribute that failure to chance, or perhaps to the whimsy of the gods, or to the obscure machinations of fate or destiny. To blame the failure on hubris, or pride, is only to apply another coat of analytical whitewash.

Though few of us live out the tragedy of our lives to such a bloody and spectacular denouement as that achieved by Oedipus, tragic failure is nonetheless a familiar pattern on all levels of society. At the top we see it in the lives of tyrants of every political stripe who are convinced that they are the beneficent servants of their harried citizens. We see it in the tyranny of fathers and mothers who with the best of intentions suffocate their children in this process called cultural filicide and then point with pride to the well-behaved, squeaky clean products of their efforts. In our adult lives we see it in the readiness with which we conform to the deadening constraints of society, a conformity which when done well we refer to as "maturity."

Freud found the female counterpart of Oedipus in Electra, who must stand passively by as her mother kills her father and then remarries. Whatever pain and ignominy Electra suffers, she was not driven to the self-destructiveness we see in Oedipus. That Freud should settle on her for his female Oedipus figure is only another indication of Freud's patriarchal bias. It is as if to say: women cannot and do not suffer as much or as grandly as we men suffer. If we set out to find a *filicidal* female equivalent of Oedipus, we find it close at hand, in the person of Jocasta, his mother. When the truth about Oedipus comes out, she exacts a greater price from herself than Oedipus does from himself. Her solution is even more violent than that of her son. So great is her guilt and so extreme her involvement that she resorts to suicide.

The Oedipal male and the Jocastan female provide us with one of the two basic sets of responses to filicidal reality: the lives of tragic failure. The other response is found in lives characterized by tragic success, in the lives of persons who pursue traditional social goals in full consciousness of what they are pursuing and who, when they achieve those goals, find only emptiness. The House of Thebes provided the model for tragic failure. The model for tragic success comes from another of the great families of Greek myth.

The House of Atreus was founded on literal filicide. Tantalus, the ancestor of Agamemnon, Orestes, and Electra, was a mortal son of Zeus, and a favorite of the gods. His special standing was lost when he committed a terrible deed: he killed his only son, Pelops, and served him at a banquet when the gods were in attendance. The gods were outraged and, after restoring Pelops to life, placed a curse on Tantalus and his descendants. Two generations later the House of Atreus produced Agamemnon.

Agamemnon and Clytemnestra have three children: Iphigenia, Electra, and Orestes. Their tragedy is set in motion at the beginning of the Trojan War. Before allowing the Greek fleet to sail for Troy, the gods demand that Agamemnon, as commander, sacrifice Iphigenia. He does so, and the fleet sails. Clytemnestra is enraged. During Agamemnon's long absence she takes a lover, Aegisthus. When Agamemnon returns from the war, Clytemnestra and Aegisthus kill him. Orestes flees, knowing that if he stays Aegisthus will murder him too. Electra is left behind to watch her mother, the murderer of her father, rule with her equally murderous consort. Electra's only hope is that Orestes will return and avenge their father's death. Which he does. Orestes kills his mother and his stepfather, because he knows it is the only thing to do. Everybody, including oracles, has been telling him as much.

The Oresteian male is the one who commits himself openly and consciously to the filicidal role of violent control. His life is characterized by tragic success. He is the man who plays by the rules and "wins." Sometimes he appears to us wearing a general's stars, sometimes wearing the Congressional Medal of Honor, sometimes wearing seven Olympic gold medals. Sometimes he amasses a financial fortune, sometimes an electoral fortune. Lesser examples abound in our lives and communities, from the local bank president on down. The Oresteian male's success becomes tragic to the extent that he becomes aware of the emotional, moral, and psychological price he pays for winning.

The woman who enjoys tragic success is Clytemnestra. Unlike Jocasta, who submits to her own guilt and to the judgment of the gods and takes her own life, Clytemnestra commits herself to vengeful action following Agamemnon's sacrifice of Iphigenia. She is aware of the price she pays in killing Agamemnon: she loses her other two children. When Orestes returns, she knows why he has come back. At that point, she no longer resists, and submits herself to his vengeance.

Tragic failure, as Oedipus/Jocasta, or tragic success, as Orestes/Clytemnestra. Those are the two basic filicidal roles open to us. Our lives, no matter how carefully and skillfully we attempt to plan and control them, are finally undercut by irony. Whom the gods would destroy, they first make filicidal.

IPHIGENIA

If we tried to find a single figure in Greek myth who most nearly perfectly embodies the tragedy of filicide, that person would surely be Iphigenia. Of all the major figures in Greek myth, she is the only one who undergoes literal, successful filicide. Euripedes changed the earlier version of the myth, so that in his telling she was saved at the last minute by divine intervention on the part of Artemis. Even spared death, her fate was not happy. Artemis transports her to Tauris, an island kingdom hostile to Greeks, where Iphigenia has to preside over the ritual sacrifice of any Greeks who fall into the hands of the Taureans. Her role in life becomes that of the accessorial mother who must aid in the sacrifice of an endless series of innocent victims. She is released from this fate only when her brother, Orestes, while trying to appease the gods for his murder of his mother, discovers Iphigenia in Tauris and takes her away with him.

Iphigenia occupies a central place both in the tragedy of the House of Atreus and in the Homeric epics. If Agamemnon had been a nonfilicidal father, he would have refused to sacrifice his daughter at the whim of the gods, which means the Greek fleet would not have sailed for Troy, which would have deprived the Greeks of their central saga of masculine violence, and we in turn would have been deprived of our two most ancient, grandest glorifications of war and its romantic after-effects. But Agamemnon is an exemplary filicidal father, to whose violence toward his child we, in a sense, owe the glories of Homer.

•

Greek myth is filled with filicide, some literal and some not. A few examples:

- At the beginning of the world, Ouranos, the creator of all things, was so repulsed by many of his children that he imprisoned them in the earth.
- Cronos ("Saturn" to the Romans) learned that one of his sons was destined to overthrow him and proceeded to eat all his children as they were born.
- That son turns out to be Zeus, who is saved through his mother's interven-

49

tion. Zeus then receives a similar warning about one of his sons and in turn reacts violently toward his offspring.

• Hercules, the man-god who does not know his own strength, kills his wife and three young sons in a fit of irrational temper. The famous Labors were a penance for those murders.

• King Acrisius learns that his daughter, Danae, will have a son who will overthrow him. Acrisius initiates a years-long persecution of Danae and her son, Perseus, whom she bears—with Zeus as the father—while she is imprisoned.

• Theseus banishes his son, Hippolytus, for allegedly being responsible for the death of Phaedra, Hippolytus' stepmother. The banishment results in Hippolytus' death.

• Procne kills her son and feeds him to her father.

• Atalanta, she who ran in the race of the golden apples, was exposed as a child because her father had wanted a son. She was rescued and raised by animals.

The farther back in time we go, the more frequent and savage the filicide tends to be. To put it the other way around: we begin history as fully developed filicides; and the more skilled we become at creating our own reality, called civilization, the farther from our consciousness our filicidal behavior recedes. Yet on deeper levels we always remain aware of what was done to us as children and what we continue to do to our own children. Mythically, the course of Western civilization may be seen in part as a gradual process in which we compulsively sought to develop a justification for our filicidal behavior adequate to the pain and guilt produced by that behavior.

As far as Greek civilization is concerned, the Oedipus-Jocasta story and the Orestes-Clytemnestra story are the two major mythic statements concerning the politics of the family. While the Greek heritage remained alive, mythically and otherwise, and furnished vital elements for the fashioning of our world, another people in another place were developing a different set of primary myths for dealing with our filicidal reality.

Whatever else the Bible contains, it is a repository of the most extraordinary evidence concerning filicide. At the same time that we were almost frantically busy developing ways to justify our filicidal behavior, we were unconsciously implicating ourselves more and more thoroughly. As in the case of the Oedipus story and the other Greek myths, we created a surface, a cover story, in the two Testaments so intricate and bizarre that we could intellectually, theologically, and emotionally wander about its metaphysical filagree and arabesques for hundreds of years without ever encountering the deadly dangers of the filicidal layer hidden beneath that finely wrought surface.

No matter how great our fear, it seems our hope is always greater. We do manage to speak the truth about ourselves, though we may do it in the most convoluted way imaginable. In these records of our beginnings it is as if we were trying to say to our future selves: *This is how it started, this civilization, this religion, this way of life, this culture, this consensual reality. It was not easy, and we had to do this and this and this in order to survive.* While many, many generations may pass before we are ready to face the truth about how we started, we record that truth in naive confidence that the day will come when we openly see ourselves for what we *were*, for that will be the day when we will have grown beyond those beginnings into new beginnings.

The filicidal record is laid out very plainly throughout the Bible. Which is to say, it becomes apparent when we are finally ready to look at it. It is most apparent in the three major beginnings:

- Genesis—in the relationship between Jehovah and Adam and Eve.
- The founding of Judaism—in the relationship between Jehovah and Abraham and Isaac.
- The founding of Christianity—in the relationship between God and Jesus and the rest of us.

The Greek myths have become more or less the playground of artists and intellectuals. The Greek perspective on human behavior touches us now for the most part indirectly. The biblical myths are still pervasive and persuasive, touching virtually all aspects of our lives, whether we find ourselves in the position of active Jew or Christian, atheist or agnostic. That this should be the case in this age of scientific enlightenment says as much about the power of our unfaced, unsolved attitudes reflected in those myths as it does about any genuine piety—or enlightenment—we may exhibit.

ADAM AND EVE

In the Eden story we have a forthright externalization of filicidal behavior, raised to the highest possible metaphysical level. The patriarchal deity creates his two children. He warns them not to eat from the tree of the knowledge of good and evil. If they do, he says, they will die. He is delivering the same coded message which filicidal parents always deliver to their children: *If you really want to be like me, you have to do what I do. Do not do what I say, even though I say you should.*

Adam and Eve eat the apple, and we get the Judeo-Christian proto-scene. Jehovah threatens them with death—and they will die eventually—but for now he settles for psychological filicide; he rejects them as unworthy creatures. They will have to survive on their own, through suffering and work. Part of the punishment is the sex-role division, which we know as "masculinity" and "femininity," and about which he is very specific. He then ejects them from his garden, because if they stay there they may eat from the tree of life and live forever. He sets up a heavy guard at the entrance to keep them out. Adam and Eve are faced with the classic children's dilemma: the problem is me *(I was disobedient)*, but the solution is outside of me *(I can be happy again only when my parents stop punishing me, which means I must behave in such a way as to be worthy of their love).*

Jehovah is a master of filicide: he controls perfectly (they leave, they suffer, they die), he is cautious (the guard at the gates), he is rational (he explains to them what will happen if they don't obey him). When they don't he rationally imposes the promised punishment.

Notice that we tell ourselves two versions of this beginning in Genesis. The first version is nonaccusatory, nonpunitive, nonfilicidal: *So God created man in his own image, in the image of God he created them; male and female he created them. And God blessed them. . . . And God saw everything that he had made, and behold, it was very good* (Genesis 1.27-28, 31). How do we get from that place of initial joy to this place of suffering? We try to explain by telling the story a second time (Genesis 2ff.). This time the story is directly accusatory—we blame ourselves for our own disobedience of Jehovah's edicts, unjustified though they may have been. It is also punitive—Jehovah places the curse of femininity on woman (painful childbirth and subservience to her husband) and the curse of masculinity on man (a life of hard work with minimal rewards).

This second version is also filicidal. Until they commit their act of disobedience, Adam and Eve are children, untouched by guilt: they are naked and unashamed of their nakedness. How do they become filicidal adults? By disobeying parental, filicidal will. After they eat the apple, Jehovah is walking through Eden looking for them. When he finds them, he asks where they were. Adam answers: *I heard the sound of thee in the garden, and I was afraid because I was naked; and I hid myself.* It is by the threat and the fact of punishment that we are cut off from the possibility and potential of love and initiated into filicidal adulthood. Fear is the weapon of filicide, and it is also the means by which our filicidal behavior is self-perpetuating. If disobedience of parental commands, which to the child may seem whimsical (what can the newborn know of death?), results in such extreme punishment, the child's consciousness can hardly contain the resulting fear. The child learns that the parent is wise and right about certain totally nonwhimsical things (touching hot stoves). Who knows what unforeseen dangers may lurk behind other nonwhimsical things which are never discussed (such as playing with the genitals of one's parents)? So we in fear submit to the cultural and sexual roles, and in fear we then impose the roles on our own children.

ABRAHAM AND ISAAC

In the covenant God makes with Abraham, the filicidal truth again comes very near to the surface of our historical consciousness. When Abraham is ninety, God appears to him and makes him an offer. If Abraham will obey God, God will 1) multiply Abraham's seed and make him "father of a multitude of nations," 2) make kings of his descendants, and 3) give him and his descendants the land of Canaan. As an outward and visible sign of the covenant, Abraham is to have himself and all his male descendants circumcised.

If the peculiar mutilation known as circumcision has any comprehensible justification behind it, practiced as it is by primitive and civilized societies all over the planet, it seems to have originally been linked with a profound male envy of the female as the ultimate source of real, biological life-power. Among primitives, circumcision is generally a part of the rite of initiation into manhood, inflicted at puberty. In that context it seems to be, individually, a masculine attempt to imitate the special role of the girl who becomes woman when blood flows from her genitals.

In the covenant with Abraham, circumcision receives authorization right from the top. It ceases to be part of the rites of puberty. Jehovah specifies that it is to be done on the eighth day after birth. Thus it ceases to be so obviously a sign of male envy of the biologically potent female. Circumcision now becomes primarily a sign of agreement between Father and his chosen Sons. The patriarchality of

Jewish circumcision is shown by the fact that:

- the male is mutilated, but not the female;
- the mutilation is of the penis, the central anatomical feature of masculinity;
- the circumcision is done on the helpless infant.

The effect is that all males become, virtually from birth, patriarchs-in-training; and they carry unmistakable evidence of their role about with them for the rest of their lives. Circumcision is the most specific and tangible of filicidal acts, short of murder. All the hidden rules and imperatives of filicide are operative in the act of circumcision. Like Oedipus' club-foot, the circumcised penis is the outward and visible sign of filicide.

Abraham keeps his side of the bargain by having himself and all males in his power circumcised. Jehovah keeps his side of the bargain first by enabling Abraham and his servant-woman, Hagar, to have a son, Ishmael, and then by enabling Abraham and his wife, Sarah, to have a son, Isaac. Both sons are circumcised. Out of jealousy, Sarah banishes Hagar and Ishmael. Abraham confers with Jehovah, who assures him a mighty race will spring from Ishmael (Mohammed will later trace his lineage back to Ishmael); so mother and son are sent packing.

This filicidal rejection of one son would be quickly overshadowed by a far worse deed imposed by divine will. The actual meaning of circumcision, the fact that it is a symbolic murder of the son, was about to be made explicit, as was the degree of obedience which a filicidal father expects from his son.

> . . .God tested Abraham, and said to him, "Abraham!" And he said,
> "Here am I." He said, "Take your son, your only son Isaac, whom you
> love, and go to the land of Moriah, and offer him there as a burnt offer-
> ing upon one of the mountains of which I shall tell you." So Abraham
> rose early in the morning, saddled his ass, and took two of his young
> men with him, and his son Isaac; and he cut the wood for the burnt
> offering, and arose and went to the place of which God had told him.
> On the third day Abraham lifted up his eyes and saw the place afar off.
> Then Abraham said to his young men, "Stay here with the ass; I and
> the lad will go yonder and worship, and come again to you." And
> Abraham took the wood of the burnt offering, and laid it on Isaac his
> son; and he took in his hand the fire and the knife. So they went both
> of them together. And Isaac said to his father Abraham, "My father!"
> And he said, "Here am I, my son." He said, "Behold, the fire and the
> wood; but where is the lamb for a burnt offering?" Abraham said,
> "God will provide himself the lamb for a burnt offering, my son." So
> they went both of them together.

When they came to the place of which God had told him, Abraham built an altar there, and laid the wood in order, and bound Isaac his son, and laid him upon the altar, upon the wood. Then Abraham put forth his hand, and took the knife to slay his son. But the angel of the Lord called to him from heaven and said, "Abraham, Abraham!" And he said, "Here am I." He said, "Do not lay your hand on the lad or do anything to him; for now I know that you fear God, seeing you have not withheld your son, your only son, from me."

The intensification of filicidal behavior throughout history consists specifically in the intensification of feelings of guilt and inadequacy on the part of the child. The person who is "parent" transfers its own unfaced, growing guilt to the person who is "child." In the Greek myths we were dealing for the most part with human parents and children. In Eden the parent was removed from this reality and seen as omnipotent deity. In the story of Abraham, things become more intense and more complicated. Abraham is both parent and child. To Isaac he is parent, and to Jehovah he is child. As God is to Abraham, Abraham is to Isaac. And: what God does to Abraham, Abraham does to Isaac. The result is that Abraham's guilt, which—to the extent that he is aware of it—he sees in terms of his failure or success in being the perfectly obedient son to God, is transferred in the most direct way possible to his son Isaac, whose life is endangered by the whole sorry process.

But it all turns out to be only a test. When God the father is convinced, by seeing Abraham holding his knife to Isaac's throat, that Abraham has learned the lesson of obedience (*. . .for now I know that you fear God*), he backs off. It is worth remembering that God the father had already given Abraham an object lesson in the administration of paternal justice by allowing him to witness and even participate in the judgment and destruction of the people of Sodom and Gomorrah. On that occasion we observe God pondering, *Shall I hide from Abraham what I am about to do. . .?* He decides not to hide his bloody judgment from Abraham, since Abraham must learn to be as much a father on earth as God is in heaven.

At this point in biblical history we had already been tested several times, and had failed to demonstrate proper fear and obedience toward the deity—at Babel, and in the Flood. Now Abraham, with Isaac's innocent if terrified aid, has passed the supreme parental test. He proves he is as much of a father as God is, and the filicidal pattern of the historical events which make up the remainder of the Old Testament is set: God commands, men disobey, God punishes. It is men primarily and not women depicted in these stories, since we were at this time busy creating a patriarchy. Anyhow, women had been written off at the beginning, as an inferior and generally unreliable source of help. In the Judeo-Christian view of things, woman's only role was that of daughter, whose cleaning and child-rearing duties—

if properly carried out—could provide some small counterbalance to her fate as eternal source of temptation to the ever-struggling men.

In the Greek stories we are for the most part innocent victims of the gods' fickleness. In the Bible we are the wayward children of God, incessantly punished for our incessant disobedience. The difference is important, because it means that as heirs of the Judeo-Christian patriarchs we find the guilt and cause of our pain and suffering (which we interpret as punishment) only in ourselves *(I am the problem)* and never in the Father-God, because he is omniscient and must therefore be a fair and righteous judge of our behavior *(. . .but the solution is outside of me)*. The implication is that we in the Bible took, and we in the present still take, the roles of parent and child, father and son, mother and daughter, very seriously. So seriously, in fact, that for us nothing else exists outside the reality circumscribed by those roles. We cannot conceive of existing in other ways, in other relationships to each other, or to the world, or to whatever God or gods may be. Such is filicide. The gentle humility of irony with its blessing of true freedom therefor eludes us as a civilization.

For us to reach the point where we find guilt only in ourselves and never in the Father-God means we have reached the point where outright, unrestrained worship of that deity begins. At that point we abdicate individual responsibility as we constantly seek the approval and pleasure of outside authority. In retrospect it is obvious that we had reached that point long before the first chapter of Genesis was written down.

This deity does not err. Any hint that this deity might act out of whimsy or maliciousness is instantly quashed by the visitation of another plague. His authority is absolute, and his administration of it is perfect. Imperfection, pain, and suffering come only from us, from our foolish, childish immaturity and our idiotic and culpable inability to carry out his crystal-clear orders. Mosaic law represents the codification—by fallible human hands, to be sure—of those orders. Since grownup sons were not yet very good at being fathers, it was necessary to attribute the orders to the highest possible source.

While Rome did the managerial work required to keep the Western world functioning on some sort of orderly basis, the responsibility for giving that world meaning thus shifted from the Greeks to the Jews. Patriarchal values which were largely implicit in Rome were in Hebraic law made explicit. The Judaic system of patriarchy, which reached its full flower in the period covered by the Old Testament, was as complete as any we have since devised, encompassing as it did both the secular and the sacred, all worlds seen and unseen. All that was lacking was the final mythic justification of the filicide which lay beneath those values.

For God so loved the world that he gave his only Son, that whoever believes in him should not perish but have eternal life. In Jesus, as we have interpreted his life and death, we attempted a total transference of our filicidal guilt to the son who is the Son of Man who is also the Son of God. It is the most grandiose of justifications of filicide, played on the largest possible stage—the entire universe, with an appropriately long run—eternity, in the most awe-inspiring form possible— the god-become-man: *Before Abraham was, I am.*

Given our filicidal needs, the Jesus story, like the Oedipal myth before it, was almost too rich in potential. As the story has come down to us, it is so patently filicidal that it is difficult to read into it anything more than the pure desperation of a race trapped in massive guilt of its own devising. The son of man indeed; and the father of us all. The biblical accounts of his life are rich in the confusion characteristic of our own filicidal lives. In one verse we find him preaching a message of breath-taking love and in the next he is reveling in condemning millions of souls to the outer darkness.

To read through one of the gospels with the theory of filicide in mind is an extra-ordinary experience. One easily senses the difficulty the writers had in grasping Jesus' message, not to mention the difficulty they had in communicating that message. What comes through is a highly garbled account of the life of a person who was preaching, and possibly living, the one message which is most dangerous and threatening to our filicidal selves and our filicidal civilization: don't hit back. In the gospels that disturbing message is surrounded and often permeated by the standard filicidal recipe for the solution of all life's problems: violence. If these earliest reports are contaminated rather thoroughly by filicidal interpretations of his deeds and parables, it is hardly surprising that in the intervening two thousand years we have turned the Jesus story almost completely to our own filicidal ends.

We have not done so consciously; because as we have been unaware of our filicide, we have also been unaware of our great need to justify it. The steady erosion of the joyous mystery embodied by Jesus has been as much an unconscious, compulsive process as our continuing flight from facing the filicidal truth about ourselves. The story was just too good for us to pass it up. What better source of additional fuel for our already blazing furnace of self-hatred than this: miserable, unworthy creatures though we children of God are, God finally deigns to send his only real son into our world. Notice that if we wanted to be accurate, we would have to speak of him as either the son of God, or the son of woman; biologically he is not the son of a man. So great is our self-hatred that we men remove ourselves com-pletely from the process. God sends his son into the world, and what happens? We kill him. Of course, the gospel writers assure us that God knew we would kill him;

even knowing that, he sent him anyway to take on the burden of human guilt, to wash away human sin in the blood of the lamb.

The knowledge that we killed the Son of God is a heavy burden, so heavy that it could more than outweigh the very guilt which filicidal Jesus was supposed to life from us. *Yes, the problem is me, but sometimes the problem gets too big to handle.* In such cases one lays the blame on another person or persons. Therefore: we didn't kill Jesus, the Jews did. They killed our God's son. But then, theological finesse has never been the long suit of institutional Christianity.

Whatever problems we had with the story, we were finally able to adjust it to fit our needs. For two thousand years a confirming echo has rolled toward us from the dark night of Golgotha as child after child after child has fallen victim to the violence of filicide; it is an echo which calms the parental mind, saying, *If God could do that to his child, then surely it is all right for me to do this to mine.* And adults have found consolation there too for their own pain and suffering: *If God could do that to his child, who am I to complain that he is doing this to me?*

Not only have we used the story to justify our own filicide, we have used it to justify a great deal of conscious homicide: *If God can kill his own son, then no one who does not share our belief in his divinity is safe before our own divinely inspired, divinely justified wrath.* So we have killed millions in wars fought explicitly or implicitly in Jesus' name. We still on occasion refer to them as holy wars.

Surely the most bizarre and revealing aspect of the very complex interpretations, rituals, and institutions based on the story of the son of God is the ritual called "communion." By eating the dead son we supposedly commune with the higher reality of his life and death. *The central ritual of the dominant religion of Western civilization is a cannibalistic celebration of filicide.* When we take communion we are justifying and celebrating God's killing of his only son, our killing of our own children, our parents' killing of ourselves, and their parents' killing of them. We kill the god of filicide and then we eat his flesh and drink his blood to convince ourselves that it is all right. At the beginning of Greek time, Cronos was doing the same thing—except he was eating his own children. The filicidal tautology is certainly true: (filicidal) human nature does not change.

The dominant image we settle on is that of crucifixion: the child of God tortured and mortified beyond endurance. Even the truly divine son cannot escape the final humiliation of filicide, that being total submissiveness to the will of the father. How we have loved to dwell on that scene through the years, in pictures and in words. To remove the familiar trappings—the grieving bystanders, the taunting soldiers, and all the rest—as Lovis Corinth did, is profoundly disturbing. We in the West were able to justify man's inhumanity to man by constructing a story of God's inhumanity to God. If that justification is removed, as Corinth did, then we are left alone with our own cruelty.

For all the harm it has done, Christianity as an organized religion contains the seeds of its own destruction. It is, after all, a son-religion, a religion whose central role is played by a non-adult, let us say. Jesus is the dutifully obedient son who, as we have depicted him, walks knowingly to his filicidal death. He despairs twice, when he asks that "this cup" should pass from him and when he feels forsaken on the cross. Otherwise, he moves directly toward his filicide. His verbal responses to his fate were generally of a forgiving sort, and have over the years proved troublesome and more than a little threatening to the patriarchal interpreters. Even more threatening were certain of his deeds, known as miracles, which tended to undercut the substance of what we think of as reality. Each of the four versions of his life shows him going about opening windows into other realities, offering glimpses of human potential which stagger our filicidal imaginations.

The final window which he opened was that of death. There he undercut the finality of filicide itself and thus robbed patriarchal and filicidal authority of any absolute or lasting importance. Notice how we turned this feat to our own filicidal ends by coming to see ultimate, absolute, and eternal authority in him *(I am the resurrection and the life; he who lives and believes in me, though he die, yet shall he live. . .).* Which is to say, if we survive death, we do so only by submitting ourselves to the authority of the murdered son and his father.

If those other realities are valid and truly open to human exploration, others will open those same windows. Human explorers by definition seek—and when they succeed in their searching, offer—liberation of one kind or another. How ironic that we should have used the discoveries by perhaps one of our greatest explorers to reinforce the prison walls. And how revealing that we should call the work of reinforcement, "deliverance." We obtain our guarantee of entry into the kingdom of heaven not through love of anyone or anything but through fear of the judgment of God and his son, through fear of punishment. After Paul and a few others were done with their editing of the story, little was left to be added except a few structural, organizational, and decorative touches. Then we were ready for generation after generation of filicidal parents and children to live out their lives of violence, fear, and hatred, made content in their discontent by the knowledge that their pain-centered behavior had been sanctioned at the highest level.

•

Organized Christianity was so adequate and sufficient a justification of our pain that it provided a framework in which Western humanity could for fifteen hundred years live out its troubled lives with only occasional and brief eruptions of internal heresy.

Filicidal reality again slips far beneath the cultural surface. During the Christian era we see the same process at work which we noted in the Old Testament following the covenant with Abraham. Everyone, poets, philosophers, politicians, preachers, all become trapped in the exploration of some variation—now simple, now elaborate—on the basic filicidal cycle of commandment-disobedience-punishment-guilt, new commandment-new disobedience, etc.

Most of the leaders whom we think of as great, attain that stature by being exceptionally clever at maintaining and acting on the culture-wide pretense that filicide does not exist. Great men are those who have led us through times of peril by using the standard filicidal solutions of violence, coercion, and war. They are men who repeatedly demonstrate to us the validity of our most tightly and fearfully held belief that the only way to win peace with honor is to fight like hell, who in other words confirm our own worst opinions of ourselves and simultaneously confirm our belief in the supreme filicidal virtues—pain and suffering. Only hard-nosed perseverance really furthers.

Similarly, much of our great art is a symbolic depiction of this experience, in which the artist accomplishes the rather difficult sleight-of-hand (actually: *trompe l'oeil*) trick of holding a mirror up to ourselves and convincing us that the image we see in the mirror is really us. What we, and it seems most artists, fail to notice is that what we see in the mirror of art is in fact an image imposed on an image which the artist unconsciously painted on the mirror before starting on the ''work of art'' itself.

Obviously the lessons of art, along with those of history, are, like those of the myths, highly ambiguous. At the same time that we have in our art and our politics and our history acted out and justified our on-going filicide, we have, as in the world of myth, continuously spoken the truth about ourselves in various hidden ways. Thus to say that Milton's *Paradise* epics, for example, are almost parodies of themselves, so unrelentingly filicidal are they, is not to imply that they are worthless. It is only to admit that certain of our cultural sacred cows are in fact steers whose potency has been somewhat overestimated by generations of adults with a vested interest in castration.

In our fear we have fallen into the habit of using what little of our potential is open to us as an excuse for avoiding the open decisions, the risk taking, the responsibility taking of continuous growth. Compulsive art-making (not to mention compulsive art-interpreting) is in this respect no different from compulsive religioning, compulsive sciencing, compulsive politicking, compulsive generaling, compulsive teaching, or compulsive working. Perhaps when we at last see the depths of our filicide and act on and beyond that insight we will discover that we can no longer art (though I suspect not). But if so, what will we have lost? Art. And what will we have gained? Life. Not a bad trade, I should think.

5. EUROPEAN MYTH

Let us back off for a moment from so strong a term as filicide with its death content and speak of the problem in other terms. The cultural roles function very much as masks, the masks of masculinity and femininity. The roles, like blinders, restrict our vision to those things, to that reality, which acculturated, civilized human beings are supposed to see. Those who succeed in dropping their masks and who survive our fear and calumny long enough to record or celebrate their new vision, we hail as geniuses. But we think the perceptions of genius are special and reserved to the "talented" few. Besides, the lives of geniuses indicate that they clearly are not normal. The possibility rarely crosses our enmasked consciousnesses that the special form of creative living which we glimpse in genius might in fact be the true human heritage which these masks are keeping us from enjoying.

Or: When filicidal behavior has ceased to have survival value, for us to continue to live and restrict our potential in the old ways is like a dancer trying to dance with a hundred pound weight attached to each foot. No one quite remembers why dancers attach hundred pound weights to their feet. It is never discussed. Now and then a dancer may appear who, because of unusual musculature or unusual will, manages an approximation of a pirouette. We in the audience gasp and applaud and tell our children and our grandchildren about it.

Or: A filicidal analysis of human behavior reveals that we are still acting as if we inhabit a frontier society, where our survival is threatened every second of every day and night, where instant obedience is required of everyone, where one mistake may be fatal not only to the individual but to the group, where there is little time for such luxuries as art, love, gentleness, or forgiveness. The internal and external barricades have to be manned at all times; and the home fires have to be womaned and kept burning at all times. Who knows what monsters lurk in that outer darkness or worse, in the inner darkness we each carry about with us? In a frontier society the dangers are real and constant, and the persons who inhabit such a place rightly have little time for paying attention to anything except those dangers. Filicidal analysis of present day society and of the roots from which this society came indicates that while many great dangers are still present, the greatest of those dangers now is us, frightenedly clinging to the old ways of violence.

In our fear we have unwittingly changed this place carved out on the frontier from the haven and place of growth which we surely meant it to be into a prison. Just as my filicidal self is at bottom a defense mechanism, my filicidal civilization is also a defense mechanism, a gigantic prison-fortress. And thus many of our so-called revolutions—political, scientific, technological, religious, philosophical, artistic, economic—are revolutionary only in that they, as Krishnamurti puts it, help us to re-arrange the furniture in the prison. For in our sleep, our death, our masks, we do not even realize we are in prison. We believe there is nothing to escape from and nothing to escape to. Prison is all.

Perhaps we have to become thoroughly entrapped, almost totally immobilized, before we can become aware of the entrapment and figure out how we got this way and what we can do about it. In the Judeo-Christian myths we saw how our depiction of filicide was raised to a higher and higher level, as if it were necessary to avoid completely any individual sense of responsibility for our cultural entrapment. In what we may perhaps term modern times, say, the period beginning with the Renaissance, the intensification continues but in a different direction. Lately the movement of "blame" has been in the opposite direction. In the ancient past, the movement was from the individual to the cosmic. In the recent past, the movement has been from the cosmic to the individual. Antiquity sought to confirm the filicidal truth: *The problem is me but the solution is outside of me.* Modernity seems intent on restating the truth in a healthier, more accurate way: *The problem is me and if there is a solution it begins with me.* An ancient insight returns. . .

HAMLET

As we construct a civilization which slowly provides more security and more leisure, we find more and more voices speaking out concerning individual experience and individual perceptions of the nature of the prison and, even, of the possibility that something may lie outside these walls of culture, language, and role. Reports of the last kind are still rare today and are viewed for the most part with skepticism, suspicion, or hostility.

In the corpus of Shakespeare's works we find countless depictions of filicidal humanity running its individual and collective heads into the walls of the prison again and again. Following many frightened glimpses through and over the ramparts of the prison in the early plays, Shakespeare at the end of his career in *The Tempest* mounted the walls and stood for a time, looking unflinchingly out over a vast, almost entirely unexplored territory. What he saw there takes us far beyond the Renaissance, indeed far beyond our own present. For his world, like ours, remained blind to what might lie beyond the walls, though the sense of entrapment was growing rapidly even then. *Hamlet* will be our case-in-point.

As soon as Freud. using the Oedipus story, points out the universality of the intense,

63

unfaced hostilities present in the members of the nuclear family, it becomes obvious to us all. We see those hostilities in our own lives and in works of art and in myths much more recent than those of the Greeks. In *Hamlet* Freud found a confirmation of his interpretation of *Oedipus.* He observed that Hamlet suffers from the same problem that afflicts the Greek hero, namely an Oedipus complex. Hamlet's mother, Gertrude, is in love with her brother-in-law, Claudius. They conspire and kill Hamlet's father, the king. To Hamlet, goaded by his father's ghost, falls the task of revenge.

What again reveals Freud's own unrealized entrapment in filicidal reality is the fact that he finds in Hamlet's paralysis, in Hamlet's inability to act forthrightly and take revenge, a confirmation not merely of the Oedipus Complex but of the *stasis* of human, Oedipal behavior. He found, in other words, a confirmation of what he took to be the fact that human nature does not change. If we look now beneath the Oedipal layer of Hamlet's behavior and explore his filicidal problems we find a revealing change has occurred. Compared with the filicidal behavior we noticed in the ancient myths, in Hamlet we find a pronounced tightening of the restraints which filicide places on us. In other words, we find evidence that the neurosis is getting worse. The primary cause of Hamlet's paralysis is not Oedipal, it is filicidal. The sense of entrapment is growing.

For Freud the main difference between Oedipus and Hamlet was the fact that Oedipus acted unconsciously while Hamlet must act in full consciousness of what he is doing. He is paralyzed because, acting in his official role as prince (heir to his real father), he must hate and take revenge on his surrogate father (the murderer of his real father) and, far worse, on his mother. The Oedipal analysis, of course, assumes—accurately—that Hamlet is in fact in love with his mother and hated his father. But his mother and her lover have, before the play begins, already done that which any Oedipal son (that being all of us sons) secretly and desperately wants to do: they have killed Hamlet's father. Thus, the Freudian reading continues, he now finds himself in a very tight spot where, as prince, he must take revenge on the one person he loves, namely, his mother. Oedipally, it is the conflict between Hamlet the son and Hamlet the prince which paralyzes him. Other hatreds are also present which grow out of the Oedipal conflict. Hamlet must on a deep level hate his mother for having done to his father that which he was unable—for whatever reason—to do. He must also hate her for having doubly betrayed him. When she removed the object of his Oedipal jealousy by murdering his father, she does not fly to Hamlet's loving arms but gives herself to another "father." And somewhere in all this emotional negativity he presumably has added another fillip of hatred toward his father for having been so stupid as to allow himself to be murdered in the first place. The result is that Hamlet cannot decide what to do, and when he at last decides, he is so confused that he botches the job, and everybody, including himself, gets killed.

64

Freud found the source of all that hatred in the basic Oedipal complex. The murderous action of the play, according to Freud, stems from the fact that the Oedipal son loves his mother and is jealous of his father. As in the Freudian reading of the Oedipus story, this interpretation is based on the unstated assumption that the two males, Hamlet and his father, relate to each other from the beginning only in a negative and competitive way. As with *Oedipus,* a filicidal reading of *Hamlet* reveals the presence of other forces.

We noted how Oedipus' life, with its reliance on violence as the appropriate solution to major problems, was determined by the attempted filicide committed on him by his parents. Whether the terrible deeds of his life are done consciously or unconsciously, the violent nature of those deeds is determined by the heritage of violence into which Oedipus is initiated as an infant. Like all filicidal sons, Oedipus is being controlled throughout by the hand of his dead father. So too with Hamlet. The difference being that Hamlet is forced to become aware of the fact that he is being controlled by the hand of his dead father. Hamlet is humanity becoming partly aware of the entrapment of filicide. The initial action of the play is the appearance of his father's ghost, who commands Hamlet to act and take revenge for his murder. Even in death his father reaches out and continues to shape and control Hamlet's life. Thus we see that, while the initial act of filicide may be confined to one proto-scene early in the life of the individual, it is, in its effects on our behavior, timeless. As long as we continue to heed the filicidal imperative, *Control,* as the only viable way of life, we are as trapped as Hamlet.

His father's ghost says to him what all parents say to all children in one way or another: *Do this violence and all will be well.* The implied specifics in what his father's ghost says to him are these: *I committed a grievous patriarchal sin—I made a mistake. I trusted your mother and I trusted my brother and sure enough, the worst happened. Now it is up to you, my son, to prove that you are a man worthy of my name. I let the situation get out of control. It is up to you to regain control. We both know the only way to do that is through violence.* The challenge to Hamlet from his father's ghost is the same challenge which all filicidal children face in times of crisis: *Be the father/mother/parent that I was supposed to be but was not.*

Hamlet is plunged into five long acts of wrestling with his fairly sensitive and gentle soul. Notice what has happened in the two thousand years since Oedipus. As civilization provides us with more security and leisure, it also prolongs that period of life known as youth. We have more and more time before we become fully committed, mature adults behaving as normal, filicidal adults are supposed to behave. Hamlet is the first prominent literary creation to speak out of the experience. His voice as he struggles with the problem of violent action versus unmanly inaction is the first echo—however faint—we have from the childhood heritage of humanity. In the famous soliloquy we are listening to the voice of an aging child whose filicidal proto-scene has not yet ended. When he says:

> To be or not to be. . .

what he is actually saying is:

> To be in the way it seems I have to be, or not to be at all.

That is the filicidal question:

> To control, or not to control—which is the same thing as to cease to
> exist.

Hamlet is trapped. He looks around and nowhere can he perceive any behavior
which might indicate that you can do anything else but control if you want to
survive. Even the escape of insanity (Ophelia) ends in death. Hamlet is the filicidal child becoming aware of what has been done to it, becoming aware of how
severely its options and choices have been restricted. So effective is filicide and so
convincing is the propaganda of filicidal civilization (otherwise known as "reality")
that we easily share Hamlet's conclusion that there are only two choices: control,
or die. The play appeals to us so strongly because we are trapped in precisely the
same way that Hamlet is trapped.

Hamlet is even deprived of the one, classic option open to the Oedipal son, that of
patricide. He can't kill his father because his father is already dead. Thus Hamlet is
the filicidal child learning that patricide, in whatever form, is a false solution. It
may yield short-term victory—Oedipus has the ambiguous pleasure of becoming his
mother's husband—but in the long-term the father's lesson of violence prevails and
you wind up dying from your own poisoned sword.

Whitehead was surely correct in his observation that all Western philosophy is only
a footnote to Plato. Wittgenstein explained how this was so when he pointed out
that we in the West are trapped in the fly-bottle of language. I would suggest that
we are also trapped in the behavioral fly-bottle of filicide. With Hamlet we begin to
become aware of that entrapment as we see that all filicidal action, however well-
intentioned, leads only to one end: destruction, of others and of self.

Hamlet obviously was not your typical patriarchal heir. Even in this age of relative
security and leisure, few of us reach the age of chronological maturity with sufficient contact left with our potential for gentleness and nonviolent living that we
even begin to question the filicidal life laid out for us. Most of us are willing and
eager to pick up the reins of control from the preceding generation of father-sons
and mother-daughters. As long as there are new worlds for us to conquer and con-

66

trol, we can most of us quite successfully ignore the fact that we are living our dead parents' lives.

One thing that will reduce us patriarchal men to unmasculine tears is the realization that there are no new worlds to conquer. Hamlet wept, but not because there were no new worlds to conquer. Hamlet wept because on some near-conscious level he saw the tragic pointlessness and meaningless repetitiveness of all compulsive conquering and controlling. Even as he wept, other males less sensitive to the filicidal dilemma were finding a vast new world to conquer and control, the world of nature. It turned out to be a world which would keep us happily and profitably occupied for the better part of four centuries.

FAUST

Science is the way of knowledge based on the predictability of predictability. As such, science is the most sophisticated expression of our desire to control. A few centuries ago we finally began to realize that things are generally more responsive to attempted control than are people. People, even in the best of circumstances, may unpredictably turn reclacitrant and upset the most carefully laid plans; the difference between the appearance and reality of French civilization will serve as an adequate example for the thoughtful reader. To take a somewhat less baroque example, let us consider the problem of government.

Government is a science only to those who teach it. To those who practice it, it is an art, and to those who must live under it, a mess. Let us narrow our focus further. Even in trying to control oneself, one can never be sure that there is not some monstrous irony hidden in the shadows of one's past which may emerge at any time and upset the whole applecart.

But with that "other" which we call nature—ah, such splendid predictability! What a fine example nature sets for us frail humans. We call the knowledge of how to control nature "science," a word which itself means "knowledge," as if that knowledge were the only knowledge worth having. And science itself has an adjunct way of knowledge called "technology," which is the way of applying the knowledge of how to control, called "science."

If we modern men are gods, and surely we are, ruling the world of women, children, and nature by unquestionable, which is to say, divine right as we do, then science and technology are our two most valuable divine servants. Is it any wonder that we have more and more turned our patriarchal backs on the clamor of the masses— the women, the children, and the lazy heathens of the rest of the world, as we isolated ourselves in our laboratories, our factories, and our offices where in peace and quiet we could ferret out the secrets of nature, building machines based on those secrets, and sell those machines for profit so that we might ferret out more secrets, build more machines to sell for profit, etc.? Even today you will find us referring to nature in the feminine. But nature is not an easy woman. She does not yield her gifts to just any suitor. To him who perseveres, to him who proves himself not only her equal but her master, her bounty is endless, her womb of a size and fecundity to match that of the infinitely long penis of our filicidal hubris. The myth of science is the basic modern myth: we treat nature like one of our own children.

If by the time of *Hamlet* we had reached a half-conscious awareness of our filicidal predicament, we had as a race also reached a kind of restless accomodation with the iron hand of our dead parents on our deadened selves. It is no surprise that, thus reduced to little more than filicidal automatons, we would turn to the world of inanimate objects as our proper sphere of activity. For creatures limited to a mindless, repetitive acting out—re-creation—of past behavior patterns, nature offers great solace, and in the bargain yields countless fascinating secrets. Western philosophies of life have generally been marked less by joy than by a certain sense of resignation and fatalism. From that sort of view to the scientific view of nature as one vast, if complex, machine was a tiny step, and a very gratifying and consoling one. How easy it is to find ourselves mirrored in nature, no matter what kind of self-image we have. Trapped within the mask of filicide, we could no longer perceive mystery, and we could no longer conceive of anything except that which we could talk about with our filicidal language and its accurate reflection of our immersion in linear time and linear causality. (A comes before B and causes B, which comes before and causes C; therefore C comes after A and is caused by A.) We turned to and embraced a cosmic determinism, which we conveniently found reflected in nature, with a fervor, passion, and enthusiasm which, I suspect, none of us knew we had left in us. It had been so long since we had resigned from the world of the freely living and creating.

We took up science with the best of intentions—to make the world safe for humanity. Blinded by our filicidal fear and hubris we continued to neglect the somewhat more difficult task of making humanity safe for the world. During our four scientific centuries we have realized a number of those good intentions, either actually or potentially. Actually, in such concrete accomplishments as the control of certain diseases. Potentially, in the development of our technological skills to the point where we now could feed, clothe, and house the world, if we just would.

In the scientific context, the theory of filicide explains why we won't, by showing that science itself, when pursued with blind compulsion, is in essence a filicidal act done to nature, the same filicidal act which we do to our children. Filicidal science as we practice it is, to coin a word, reicide: the murder of things. Now,

68

even as the whole beautiful, reductive structure of science and technology begins to collapse on top of us, as the force and violence we have used to extract and apply the laws of nature begin to turn on us, we still fail to see any relationship between the external tragedy and the internal, hidden lives of all humans. To be sure, religious voices of doom fill the land with reminders of our inner corruption, but they wish us only to exchange our submissiveness to science for our older submissiveness to the superannuated gods of their secularized religions. Filicidal humanity is like a compulsive rapist who can see no connection between his external violence and the darkly confused quality of his inner experience.

For example, the theory of filicide illuminates the following irony. The three laws of thermodynamics, articulated in the nineteenth century, are one of the capstones of patriarchal science. The second of those laws, the so-called entropy law, states in effect that the universe is running down ("entropy" means "turning in on itself"). The universe is perceived as a gigantic heat-energy machine. It became clear to observers of that machine that energy was constantly being consumed in the various activities and transformations so apparent in the universe. It was also clear, the observers felt, that there was no external source of additional energy. Therefore the heat-death of the universe must be inevitable. Eventually all these particles, atoms, and molecules so busily rotating and vibrating will reach a state of maximum disorder in which all activity will cease and the universe will be at rest. Creatures whose lives are firmly rooted in death, who can find meaning only in action, and for whom life itself is a losing struggle against death, can obviously find only death when they observe things outside of themselves. As we noted at the outset, at the end of filicidal history is, literally, nothing. At the end of filicidal science we also find nothing—surcease, total paralysis at absolute zero.

Obviously the laws of thermodynamics have a certain validity. Our understanding of them has made it possible to build a fairly reliable refrigerator (although the laws behind the construction of a reliable digital watch continue to elude us). The point is that such laws, when interpreted to have absolute, universal, and eternal validity, are clearly an externalization of the dead lives led by the men who derived and interpreted the laws. Certainly one of the more encouraging signs in the modern age has been the occasional note of confused humility sounded lately by this or that mandarin of twentieth century physics.

To bring the entropy argument a bit closer to home: The energy problems of the late modern era served as confirmation in more than one quarter of our fatalistic theories of nature. Sure enough, the world was running down. We failed to see that there might be a significant connection between the energy crisis and such other end-of-an-age phenomena as the catastrophe of Vietnam (where filicidal patriarchs could not find the internal energy to do the classic, dirty job of unrestrained war once again), the death of God-as-we-have-known-and-feared-him, and certain confusions in other areas of civilized reality.

Those of us who are well settled into that reality and have a strong vested interest (otherwise known as "personality") in its continuation are frightened by a growing sense of helplessness (who is in control here?) and frightened again as we observe disturbingly large amounts of creative energy in persons who seem to be behaving in at least partial disobedience to the old ways, such as those persons whom we see in various ethnic, political, and sex-role liberation groups. Where does their energy come from? Could it be that there is more than one universe? Could it be that not all universes suffer heat-death?

We don't formulate such questions. We choose rather to fight, thereby to demonstrate to those persons and to ourselves that, by God, we still have it in us to control as well as our ancestors did. As we fight, we find even in our death throes a confirmation of our worst fears rather than finding reason to re-examine our most basic, hidden assumptions about ourselves.

Where the old institutions show some signs of life, we read the signs only as a further contribution to the general, growing chaos. Organized science throws up an uncertainty principle. Organized religion makes some spasmodic moves in the direction of seeing sex as something other than dirty. Capitalistic government hints at an awareness that hunger may not necessarily be divine punishment for Original Laziness. Communist government hints at an awareness that freedom of speech might actually aid the realization of production goals, and so on. But cowering in the filicidal darkness we keep our eyes closed to doubly shut out the light. We thus ignore even the occasional signs of growth, or we recoil in terror before them if we do take cognizance of their existence—popular reactions to the gay movement being a case-in-point.

We are now so completely immersed in a death-oriented civilization that it is almost trite to speak of that fact. If not trite, then hopeless. Hopelessness is, after all, the very goal our filicidal, familial, religious, scientific selves are most comfortable with. Perhaps the real filicidal imperative is coded. Perhaps when we say, *Control,* what we actually mean is, *Do everything you can to try to control but you know of course that you're going to lose in the end anyway.* The purest of the sciences—mathematics and physics—unite to give us a planetary time bomb in the form of thousands of nuclear warheads scattered about the globe. And the official journal of the scientists who created that time bomb conveniently provides a clock on its cover. The hands of the clock are dutifully adjusted backward or forward a few seconds each issue so that we may have some idea of how close we are to the nuclear midnight when all the bombs go off. Scientists and others who try to do something about the nuclear armageddon are labeled un-American, un-Russian, un-Chinese, or whatever, and lose their security clearances—or worse.

In the first seventy-five years of the twentieth century we kill well over one hundred million people in wars and we persist in seeing ours as a civilization of progress. An American president releases the most devastating bombing raids in history and describes them as the beginning of a generation of peace.

Surrounded by humanly inflicted violent deaths, we take note of the fact but find in it only confirmation of our worst fears and beliefs concerning ourselves. In such a world, we conclude with exemplary fatalism, you can't trust anybody, not even yourself. All you can do is try to exert maximum control at all times. Those deaths were the other person's fault, the fault of all those other persons known as the enemy. A hundred million deaths only offer convincing evidence of how dangerous and widespread the enemy is.

As long as we remain trapped within the narrow confines of our filicidal personalities with their one goal of perfect control, we will continue to find adequate enemies "out there," whether in the form of animals, things, or people.

Thousands of years of filicidal behavior at last got us to the place emotionally where, in *Hamlet*, we could fairly accurately depict the death-like paralysis in which we exist. As we embraced the scientific way of knowledge with some very good intentions, we were simultaneously continuing our flight from the inner truth about our filicidal selves. The more attention we paid to controlling the world of things, the less attention we paid to our responsibility for knowing or not knowing ourselves for what we are. The intensification of the filicidal paralysis brought with it an intensification of the patriarchality of our civilization, of our very reality, in the rise to power of the bourgeoisie. To be born female came more and more to mean that one was born into slavery. If born a woman in the right place, at the right time, with the right skin color, you might have a life of quite comfortable slavery, but it was still a life of slavery. To be born male came more and more to mean that one was born into the ruling class.

The whole process of patriarchality reached a climax in the creation of the bourgeois household, with its nuclear family nestled snugly into a vast set of laws designed to protect the rights of the master of the household as he lorded it over his wife and children. Our successful demonstration of our cleverness and potency through science and technology enabled us to create a patriarchy whose near-perfection rivaled that of the Old Testament sages.

In the myths of the modern age, those of, say, the last two centuries, women have almost totally disappeared from view. So securely did we have women locked away in the bourgeois castle that, when a female figure does surface in one of the modern myths, she does so in the most bizarre and extreme way. An analysis of these myths reflects this gross sexual imbalance. In a world as intensely and compulsively and frightenedly masculine as this one, it is no surprise that the filicidal myths that world has created are also intensely and compulsively and frightenedly masculine.

•

The closer we come to the present, the greater the difficulty in selecting the significant myths. It is the stories that we tell and re-tell and then tell again that are, as it were, a dead give-away. They are the ones most likely to contain truths about ourselves that we are not quite ready to face openly.

If we want to delve beneath the handsome surface of filicidal science, one story presents itself as the obvious candidate, that being the Faust legend, with its countless re-tellings. Of these the grandest is Goethe's epic version, in which we find an aging scientist so desperate for knowledge that he is willing to sell his soul to the Devil in exchange for the real knowledge which has eluded him in the laboratory.

Goethe's *Faust* suffers from the same shortcoming, in filicidal terms, which one encounters in many of our greatest literary creations. Author and characters are so submerged in filicidal reality that they can show us everything except themselves—and thus ourselves as well. With insight and beauty Goethe reveals to us Faust's insatiable desire for knowledge. The dilemma, as Goethe puts it, is that Faust in his desperate striving has done a great deal of good (developing a cure for the plague, for example), but he has never found contentment. In the pact with Mephistopheles Faust observes that he has never experienced a moment which was so nearly sufficient to his needs and desires that he would have wanted that moment to extend itself in time. If Mephistopheles can enable Faust to experience such a moment, Faust is quite willing for him to have his soul. Whatever his degree of filicidal blindness, Faust is at least aware that the control gained from science is only another fleeting illusion. To that extent he already stands outside of filicidal reality as the epic begins.

For some 12,000 lines we follow this strange pair through all the worlds, visible and invisible, as Mephistopheles tries to seduce Faust into contentment. It is a grand tour of the universe, through sex, witchcraft, the spirit world, everything. But nowhere does Faust find the knowledge to make him content. At the end they return to earth and Faust turns to philanthropy. He applies his knowledge of science and technology to a land reclamation project in the Netherlands.

At last he stands looking out over the pastoral scene he has helped create from an area which was once the bed of the ocean, and he says to Mephistopheles that the sight almost might make him say to the moment of viewing: "Tarry a while." "Might," indeed. Mephistopheles overlooks Faust's hedging use of the subjunctive, decides that he has won, and prepares to whisk Faust off to hell—only to be interrupted by God. It turns out the dice were loaded from the beginning, against Mephistopheles. We learn that God understands and approves our incessant struggle to control. It is man's nature, God says, to strive, and as long as man strives, he will err. At the end of Faust's—and our—long road of suffering lies only forgiveness, not damnation. God forgives Faust and admits him to the glories of heavenly surcease, or whatever.

In a sense Goethe's epic depiction of the human situation thus transcends the killing limits of filicidal self-hatred. It is in fact the same humanitarian place of compassionate understanding which in some way, sacred or secular, we all want to believe exists as a kind of ultimate reality, the place where even without knowing all, we can forgive all. It is much the same place where Oedipus winds up in *Oedipus at Colonus,* the sequel to *Oedipus Rex.* We keep alive the truth concerning the possibility of mercy in much the same way we keep alive other truths we cannot yet face. Goethe says that, yes, forgiveness comes finally, but to reach that end we have no choice but to suffer and to cause suffering through the long years of our controlling lives. Goethe's view may be somewhat more hopeful than, say, that of Shakespeare, but it is still focused on the compulsive striving for control which characterizes filicidal behavior. The problem for Hamlet was: control *or* die. For Faust the problem is: control *and then* die. Not just die, but die happy.

Thus *Faust,* for all its extraordinary qualities, is constructed on an implicit acceptance of the filicidal inability to relax and let go as a part of, well, human nature. Goethe's epic is yet another example of that deceptive process mentioned earlier — the artist holds up a mirror to humanity and neither the artist nor we notice that in addition to the images reflected in the mirror we are also seeing an image which is part of the mirror itself.

FRANKENSTEIN

If *Faust* will not serve as a modern filicidal touchstone, we look elsewhere and find such a touchstone in a rather unlikely place, hidden away in the original version of one of the most famous and frequently re-told of all modern stories: *Frankenstein,* by Mary Wollstonecraft Shelley.

Shelley's "monster novel," itself a re-telling of one of humanity's oldest myths— that of the creation of life, turns out to contain the most explicit and detailed representation of the filicidal politics of the patriarchal family that we have available. It is probably no accident that the creator of the definitive depiction of filicidal reality behind modern patriarchal behavior was a woman. By the beginning of the nineteenth century, men had yielded so nearly totally to the seductive pursuit of the rewards for well-practiced control—money, power, and prestige—that we had almost completely lost touch with our humanity.

Shelley, her husband, Percy, and Byron spent a long, somewhat dreary summer in Switzerland in 1816. As Shelley tells the story in her introduction to *Frankenstein,* there had been much talk in the little group concerning the supernatural, the origin of life, and the recent discoveries in the use of electricity. They had also been reading various German ghost stories. At length they decided on a competition. Each was to compose a supernatural story of some kind for the entertainment of the others. They set to work, but Byron and Percy quickly tired of such an unworthy application of their Olympian talents and turned back to the loftier pursuits of poetry. Mary persevered. For several months she persevered. Between caring for her infant son and her grown-up poet-husband, the writing down of *Frankenstein* was a matter of a moment stolen here and another stolen there. The novel was finished and sent off to a London publisher who brought it out in 1818. It was an immediate success and has remained popular ever since as a classic of "horror fiction." And of course the fame of the book has been compounded many times by innumerable stage, movie, and television adaptations.

Why should this rather simple horror story have intrigued so many for so long? For one thing, *Frankenstein* is a good story well-told. With a sure economy of words (the novel runs to only some 200 pages), which certain more famous male persons close to her might have done well to emulate, Shelley gave the handful of central characters a depth and richness which a long series of adaptors have neither matched nor exhausted. Even with its somewhat archaic rhetoric, its occasionally creaking plot, its excess of sentiment, the novel still comes off extraordinarily well. The frequently ill-guided excisions, abbreviations, and additions to which generations of would-be adaptors have resorted only show that Shelley understood the story far better than they—and perhaps the rest of us as well.

But no matter how well written, a novel achieves the kind of enduring popularity which *Frankenstein* has enjoyed only if it strikes a strong, resonant chord in large numbers of readers. What chord is it this novel has continued to strike for over a century and a half? There are at least two, one obvious and one not so obvious.

The obvious: *Frankenstein* was the first novel to exploit and explore successfully our fascination with the new god, Science, its attendant promises and dangers. The book bears the subtitle: *The Modern Prometheus.* Victor Frankenstein is just that, a new Prometheus in the form of the scientist who brings fire—the spark of life—to humanity by creating life itself. As Shelley unfolds the story she reveals to us the irony in the subtitle and thus the irony in science itself. With the best and noblest of intentions Frankenstein sets out to create another human being. He speaks of his task as a means for conquering death and the debilitating effects of various

74

diseases, but he winds up creating Death itself as his creation, a monster of great strength and equally great rage, turns on him and his family. Where the mythological Prometheus was a savior of humanity, this new Prometheus becomes a destroyer of humanity, or at least of Victor's familial portion of humanity. At the same time that the novel appeals to our rather childish belief in the omnipotence of science, it also plays on our fear and distrust of such a potent "god." Shelley thus created the basic formula used with great success and profit by countless imitators ever since. We are both fascinated and frightened by the scientist and by the scientist's creations.

The less obvious chord *Frankenstein* strikes is filicidal. Shelley has here given us a woman's report on how filicidal, patriarchal humanity looked in the early nineteenth century. It is not a pretty picture, nor is it, it turns out, a very dated one. We see our modern selves, particularly our masculine selves, reflected with an accuracy and a realism often lacking in male-authored modern myths. The novel is in effect a slave's barely disguised report on the real behavior of the master race. That behavior stands in stark contrast to the pretended behavior of the masters as one generally finds it described in their own self-serving stories about themselves.

Victor Frankenstein, a spoiled and pampered son of an upper-class Swiss family, compulsively driven to solve the mystery of life, creates another male, a "son." He is therefore the perfect filicidal father. He does not need a woman to create his son. (Compare the similar behavior of the Judeo-Christian God in Eden.) At the moment of animation of his creation, Victor's enthusiasm ("love") changes to revulsion and in a dreadful proto-scene he rejects his "son" as a monster and flees in terror. The son, whose mind is initially as unformed and open as that of an infant is left to stumble about the countryside, desperately seeking love but engendering fear and violence in everyone he encounters. When father and son at last meet again, there is still hope. The son is not yet totally committed to a life of violent control—if Victor could find it in himself to show any emotion besides terror and revulsion, the son might learn that some kind of masculine behavior other than that of violent control is possible. Victor does not. In fact he betrays what little trust his son has in him. The son then turns to vengeful murder, seeking out the members of Victor's family, and finally Victor himself. Father and son pursue one another across the world until they finally achieve the ultimate filicidal success—mutal self-destruction.

We think we know the story so well. Just as the Greeks thought they knew the story of Oedipus quite well: the scientist alone in his laboratory, face to face with the biggest mother of them all, Mother Nature. Note, in passing, how the Japanese reduced the story to its essence. In the Godzilla re-tellings, the monster becomes both hero and villain. And all humanity is sacrificed in the bottomless maw of the monster. We who in an earlier age were cannon fodder have in the age of science become monster fodder. We keep on seeing the monster as the Son of Science, failing to realize that Science is us and that scientific behavior is only the latest of our attempts at control. So we dismiss these stories as childish, foolish nonsense, the stuff of dreams and nightmares. Indeed. Since as a society we are in the habit of ignoring our dreams, it is no surprise that we have so easily consigned Mary Shelley's particular dream to the world of irrelevant fantasy.

•

Frankenstein: The New Prometheus begins in one of the most desolate parts of the world, the arctic icecap. In a series of letters to his sister in England, Robert Walton describes his expedition to find the northwest passage. In a kind of adumbration of the later development we will see in the main character of the novel, Walton speaks of the compulsion which drove him to mount such a dangerous undertaking. Also, as Frankenstein will later do, he refers to his feeling that some hidden destiny is controlling him. And he feels isolated—he longs for a friend. He, as commander, cannot be friends with the crew of his ship. He must be their captain, their father, he says.

He describes an apparition who appears one day, more dead than alive, stumbling across the ice. Half-frozen, the person is taken aboard and revived. It is Victor Frankenstein in the final pursuit of his monstrous creation—though he doesn't admit this to his rescuers. When they ask how he came to be in such a place he says only that he is there to "seek one who fled me." When Walton tells Victor that they had recently seen another, huge figure moving across the ice, Victor becomes excited but refuses to explain the situation. Days pass and Victor spends all his time on deck, constantly scanning the endless ice. To use Shelley's rhetoric: a bond of affection develops between Walton and Frankenstein. They are after all brothers-in-compulsion. As time passes with no further sign of his creation, Victor sinks into despair.

Walton gently goads him into telling his story. The main body of the novel ensues. Each night after Frankenstein has gone to sleep, Walton records the tale as he remembers it, to send to his sister. Thus the bulk of the novel is a frame-story, a common device for making a fantastic story more believable to the reader. The device also gives the appearance of removing the writer one step from direct responsibility for the story—a fact of more than scholarly interest since the novel eventually turns into a story within a story within a story within a story. Hidden in that fourth level we will find the one fairly well-developed female character in the book, a character who bears more than a little resemblance to Mary Shelley.

So Victor Frankenstein begins his story.

His father married late. His mother was the daughter of his father's recently deceased, poverty-stricken best friend. The couple spent several years traveling. Victor was born in Naples. He describes his childhood as idyllic:

> *I was their plaything and idol. . . During every hour of my infant life I received a lesson of patience, of charity, and of self-control. . . .*

Here and throughout the book it is obvious that Victor idolizes his parents as much as he believes they idolized him.

When he was five, the family was vacationing at Lake Como, where his mother befriended one Elizabeth Lavenza, the young orphan daughter of a bankrupt Italian aristocrat. Victor's parents bring Elizabeth home one day and introduce her to Victor as "a pretty present." As soon as Victor saw her, he:

> *looked upon Elizabeth as mine—mine to protect, love, and cherish. All praises bestowed on her I received as made to a posssession of my own. We called each other familiarly by the name of cousin. No word, no expression could body forth the kind of relation in which she stood to me—my more than sister, since till death she was to be mine only.*

That is the way Victor treats Elizabeth for the course of the book, as his prized possession, and as his better half. She has in abundance all those virtues which he lacks—patience, open affection, consistent tenderness, sensitivity to the effect of one's actions on others. She is in other words the ideal and idealized woman—and wife. Though they do not marry till near the end of the story—and then their union ends quickly and tragically—this chaste pair serves as the ideal, asexual parents of Victor's monster-son. Victor, as the ultimate father, does not need to copulate with woman to create new life. He'd rather do it himself. And he does. But no matter where his studies and the awesome result of his studies take him, Elizabeth is always back in Geneva, keeping the homefires burning for her less-than-husband-but-more-than-brother, whenever he may find it advantageous to return to her. She is the stabilizing, emotionally secure anchor which enables the man in her life to get out there and succeed, always knowing that he has her to come home to.

Victor is no fool. He is aware of the differences between himself and Elizabeth, is aware of her sensitivity and to some extent is aware of his own lack of sensitivity. But, he tells Walton:

> *While my companion contemplated with a serious and satisfied spirit the magnificent appearances of things, I delighted in investigating their causes. . . The world was to me a secret which I desired to divine. Curiosity, earnest research to learn the hidden laws of nature, gladness*

akin to rapture, as they were unfolded to me, are among the earliest sensations I can remember.

With that, the two major themes of the novel are stated. The scientific theme, which will drive Victor to create his own son, and the filicidal theme of compulsive control, which will drive him to destroy his son and himself. His parents saw him as their plaything, but they were traditional parents, meaning filicidal parents. They also saw him as:

> *their child, the innocent and helpless creature bestowed on them by heaven, whom to bring up to good, and whose future lot it was in their hands to direct to happiness or misery, according as they fulfilled their duties towards me.*

It is precisely that sense of compulsive, controlling parental duty which will be the undoing of both creator and created as the story unfolds. Reflected in that attitude is the inability to allow the child to learn to accept responsibility for its own deeds which, as we have already seen, lies at the heart of filicidal behavior.

As a youth, Victor has one close friend other than his de facto wife-to-be. He is very drawn to a schoolmate, Henry Clerval, who is on the surface anyway a kind of male version of Elizabeth. Where Victor is driven to find the secrets of nature, Henry spends his time contemplating the surface of nature and pondering the "moral relations of things." (Obviously there is also a biographical level to the novel, of which scholars have made much; Victor can be seen as a broadly drawn portrait of Byron. Elizabeth is a reflection of Byron's half-sister with whom he may or may not have had a sexual relationship. Henry of course is Percy Shelley.)

With Henry on stage all the main characters are present—except one. In a masterful bit of plotting, Shelley keeps the last and crucial character offstange untilalmost halfway through the book. The monster is created long before that but is then set loose in the countryside, and we are left to our own imaginative devices concerning what he may be doing while Victor sits around wringing his (and of course Elizabeth's and Henry's) hands. Anyhow, with these three characters, the stage is set. Victor grows up attracted to science or, as it was known at the time, natural philosophy. He gets off on the wrong track for a while by reading the alchemists. Then he goes to an Austrian university where a few modern chemistry professors set him straight. Victor, it turns out, is a fast learner. Within two years he has assimilated all that the university has to offer. He sets up his own laboratory, in hot pursuit of the secret of life.

During this time he is aware that something is compelling him, but he can do nothing about it. In his first interview at the Austrian university, the professor ignites Victor's young soul with his praise of the wonders of science. Victor recalls the professors's little speech as "the words of fate":

> One by one the various keys were touched which formed the mechanism of my being; chord after chord was sounded, and soon my mind was filled with one thought, one conception, one purpose. . . . [to] pioneer a new way, explore unknown powers, and unfold to the world the deepest mysteries of creation.

As men are wont to do, whether seeking a polio vaccine, an atomic bomb, or success in the business world, Victor drives himself mercilessly in his quest for the secret of life. He even stops writing home to Geneva. His efforts pay off. Soon enough he discovers the "cause of generation and life," a discovery which he feels is reward enough for any difficulties caused by his compulsion.

> . . .with how many things are we upon the brink of becoming acquainted, if cowardice or carelessness did not restrain our inquiries.

Having discovered the secret of life, Victor is faced with the problem of what to do with it. He interrupts his narration here to scold Walton when Walton asks him just what that secret consists of. After a brief sermon from Victor, Walton retreats and the story continues. Victor decides he will make—what else—a man. In fact he will make a man bigger than life. Because of the delicacy of many of the necessary operations, he will construct his man about a third larger than life, which is to say, about eight feet tall.

There we have a detail which opens up some intriguing possibilities. Certainly if one is writing a novel about a monster, one way to make the monster frightening is to make it very large. There may be more involved here. Perhaps Shelley, through Victor, is creating man as he appears to women. To female children Daddy is of course bigger than they are. Even when they grow up he is still bigger. Another possibility is that Shelley is here creating the forbidden childhood memory of Father as the very large, omnipotent filicide who, even when we—whatever our sex—grow up, remains psychologically just enough bigger that he continues to be a threatening and controlling influence in our lives.

Which brings us to the heart of the novel: the first meeting between father and son, the playing out of the proto-scene when Victor animates his creation.

The scene (Chapter 5) was, significantly, written first. Shelley tells us in the introduction to the novel that after she wrote this scene she was thinking of leaving it in that form as a short piece of fiction. It was at Percy's suggestion that she began turning it into a novel. Also in the introduction she offers some revealing remarks concerning the origin of this central scene. Her little group had been reading aloud German ghost stories. She summarizes the plot of one of these which, in this filicidal context, is rather striking. The story concerned

> the sinful founder of his race whose miserable doom it was to bestow the kiss of death on all the younger sons of his fated house, just when they reached the age of promise.

Shelley reproduces the climactic scene:

> His gigantic, shadowy form, clothed like the ghost in Hamlet, in complete armor, but with the beaver up, was seen at midnight, by the moon's fitful beams, to advance slowly along the gloomy avenue. The shape was lost beneath the shadow of the castle walls; but soon a gate swung back, a step was heard, the door of the chamber opened, and he advanced to the couch of the blooming youths, cradled in healthy sleep. Eternal sorrow sat upon his face as he bent down and kissed the forehead of the boys, who from that hour withered like flowers snapped from the stalk.

In its way the story is an even more poignant reflection of filicidal reality than is Shelley's novel—this father's very kisses are fatal. One can also wonder at the fact that Shelley for some reason felt it necessary to tell us about having read this particular story. Another indication, perhaps, that she was aware that her novel was concerned with much more than demonstrating the irony and dangers of the new promethean science.

Adding to the evidence that Shelley was working here from the very deep layers of human perception and motivation is the fact that the central scene of *Frankenstein* came to her as a dream. When the group had decided on its little writing competition, the men at once set about to work on their stories. A fourth person was involved, a certain Dr. Polidori, whose vampire tale would become the model for Bram Stoker's classic *Dracula* half a century later. Shelley had trouble getting started. She couldn't think of a proper beginning for her story. One night the group had been talking about electricity, specifically about the possible creation of life using electricity. Shelley tells us in her introduction what then happened.

> Night waned upon this talk, and even the witching hour had gone by before we retired to rest. When I placed my head on my pillow I did not sleep, nor could I be said to think. My imagination, unbidden, possessed and guided me, gifting the successive images that arose in my mind with a vividness far beyond the usual bounds of reverie. I saw—with shut eyes, but acute mental vision—I saw the pale student of un-

> *hallowed arts kneeling beside the thing he had put together. I saw the hideous phantasm of a man stretched out, and then, on the working of some powerful engine, show signs of life and stir with an uneasy, half-vital motion. Frightful it must be, for supremely frightful would be the effect of any human endeavor to mock the stupendous mechanism of the Creator of the world. His success would terrify the artist; he would rush away from his odious handiwork, horror-stricken. He would hope that, left to itself, the slight spark of life which he had communicated would fade, that this thing which had received such imperfect animation would subside into dead matter, and he might sleep in the belief that the silence of the grave would quench forever the transient existence of the hideous corpse which he had looked upon as the cradle of life. He sleeps; but he is awakened; he opens his eyes; behold, the horrid thing stands at his bedside, opening his curtains and looking on him with yellow, watery, but speculative eyes.*

Thus was the modern myth of Frankenstein's monster born in a hypnogogic vision of Mary Shelley. And thus was born Mary Shelley's attempt to break the ultimate taboo of a filifical society: to see and report on the reality of the proto-scene. Thus began the saga of *Frankenstein,* a childish horror story whose ending we are, it seems, still in the process of devising.

The proto-scene of the novel: adult Father. physically mature, wise, skilled, omniscient, meets newborn Son, physically malformed, ignorant, clumsy, naive. Father, who until that moment of face-to-face meeting had been able to keep himself going with an idealized internal picture of Son as beautiful and perfect, is suddenly faced with the reality of this male person whom he has created. When Victor animates his son, the son hardly stirs, but Victor's disillusionment is immediate and total:

> *His yellow skin scarcely covered the work of muscles and arteries beneath; his hair was of a lustrous black, and flowing; his teeth of a pearly whiteness; but these luxuriences only formed a more horrid contrast with his watery eyes, that seemed almost of the same color as the dun-white sockets in which they were set, his shriveled complexion and straight black lips.*

One assumes that the nonphysical, transcendent God of the Bible had thought that he had created beautiful children. One assumes that that nonphysical creator found the behavior of those two children as ugly as Victor finds his son's physical appearance. Both creators react in similar ways. Of course it does not befit a patriarchal deity to flee, so God commands his creations to flee. Victor, being something less than a transcendent deity, has to do the fleeing himself, which he does. In passing we should note another similarity to the Eden story. When circumstances

81

later bring Victor and his creation together, Victor's standard response to his son's repeated requests for help is a lofty and Jehovah-like, "Begone!" The lesson being that you should make sure that you are either bigger than your creation or that you so intimidate your creation that it thinks you are bigger.

Victor rejects his son and flees. He goes to an inn near his laboratory in the little Austrian town where he has been working and spends a restless night. He is engulfed by two emotions: terror and despair. One wonders if his despair is not a kind of masculine post-partum depression. He describes his feelings:

> . . .dreams that had been my food and pleasant rest for so long a space were now become a hell to me; and the change was so rapid, the overthrow so complete!

Or is he perhaps merely suffering the classic, patriarchal, post-copulative let-down (Victor after all has just come like no man has ever come before him) which men have been complaining about since antiquity?

Are we to see in Victor's response to the sight of his living creation some kind of automatic paternal rejection syndrome? Is is possible that we have been being killed by our parents so long that filicide has become if not an instinct at least a deeply ingrained, learned response to one's child? We learn later, from the monster himself, that at his "birth" he, like any newborn, was perceiving what was going on around him, but only very vaguely. He later tells Victor that he knew he had been left alone (exposed on the mountainside, as it were), but at the time was not aware of the intensity of Victor's feelings. So that Victor, if he could have found it in himself to love, could have repaired much of the emotional damage done by this initial rejection. But Victor, as a man, can behave only as a man behaves, which is to say, filicidally. He is caught in the same trap with Oedipus and Hamlet.

Next morning, following Victor's fear-filled night at the inn, Shelley contrives to bring his old friend, Henry Clerval, into the lobby as Victor is passing through. Henry has come from Geneva to find out why Victor hasn't been writing. Victor's relief is enormous at the sight of his friend, but he doesn't tell Henry what is going on. With Henry to lean on, Victor returns to his laboratory. It is empty. As Victor puts it to Walton: ". . .my enemy had indeed fled." His son has been alive less than a day and already is his enemy. Victor is literally wild with joy to find his creation gone. Henry is puzzled but Victor tells him nothing. Victor's emotions are so intense that he collapses and remains in a semi-conscious state for several months.

A year passes during which Victor regains his sanity. He manages to put the monster completely out of his consciousness and represses his former life so completely that he develops a "violent antipathy even to the name" of science. But the relationship between this father and his monstrous son has hardly begun. A letter arrives from Victor's father with the news that Victor's young brother, five-year-old William, has been murdered. Victor returns to Geneva and before going home visits the spot where his father said William was killed. A thunderstorm is raging. As Victor contemplates the spot a flash of lightning reveals an unmistakable, giant figure stealing off through the bushes.

In that moment of terror everything falls into place for Victor. His memories return and he relives his suppressed past. Although he cannot imagine how it came about, he must assume that his own son was the murderer of William. He has a sudden insight into the reality of his life as he perceives that his creation is in fact his own "vampire, my own spirit let loose from the grave and forced to destroy all that was dear to me." Several times in the future Victor will come up against this insight, but it is always too much for him to accept. He cannot face the part of himself which seems so creative and clever but which is in reality so destructive. That which he cannot accept, he hates. Notice that this son who is the father, this "vampire" which is Victor's creation, remains nameless—that is perhaps the most serious rejection of all in this patrilinear society where one of the keystones of the masculine personality is the "immortality" gained through the imposition of one's name on one's wife and children. Victor cannot recognize his son's paternity. There is an ironic bit of folk wisdom in the fact that the name "Frankenstein" is now popularly understood to refer to the monster-son and not to the father.

In despair Victor returns to his mourning family. The plot creaks badly at this point. Another of the Frankenstein family's adoptive daughters, Justine, is tried for the murder of William on the basis of circumstantial evidence. This is Shelley tightening the vise on Victor seemingly to the breaking point, but of course the worst is yet to come. Victor wrestles with his conscience. If he tells the truth, no one will believe him. But even if his story is believed, Victor is certain the monster would wreak terrible vengenace if pursued. Thus Victor remains silent. After Justine is convicted Victor and Elizabeth visit her in prison. Elizabeth is miserable but Victor realizes that she suffers the misery of innocence in the presence of atrocity while he suffers the misery of guilt. Justine is executed, and Victor realizes the double bind in which he is trapped. If he remains alive he will have to bear the torment of his guilt. If he kills himself he is certain the monster would go on a rampage of destruction. Such is the filicide's burden, here again, as it was for Hamlet: to live successfully means to control successfully.

Frankenstein's sense of guilt is further increased as he compares the failure of his own life with his father's "serene conscience and guiltless life." That his mild-mannered, gentle-voiced father might have been responsible for initiating Victor into the filicidal life of violent control at an early age is so inconceivable a possibility that it is not considered. *The problem is me.* Or that Elizabeth, in her pristine innocence, might somehow be playing a passive, accessorial role is equally inconceivable. As she says to Victor: where, before, the terrors of the world of men were

> *remote and more familiar to reason than to the imagination. . . now misery has come home, and men appear to me as monsters thirsting for each other's blood.*

She is as thoroughly trapped in her filicidal woman's role as Victor is in his man's role. She at least establishes the equation:

$$men = monsters.$$

But it is a long step from that to the more accurate statement of the equation:

$$filicidal \ men = monsters,$$

with its implication that men can perhaps cease being monsters by ceasing to be filicidal. And it is an even longer step to the final equation of traditional family politics:

$$filicidal \ humanity = monsters,$$

which implicates both sexes at the same time that it offers hope for release for both sexes.

Victor's reaction to his half-sister's words is predictably filicidal:

> *I listened to this discourse with extremest agony. I, not in deed, but in effect, was the true murderer.*

Of course he does not mean he is responsible for turning his son into a murderer. Behind his statement lies the unspoken filicidal syllogism:

> 1. I created a son.
> 2. All sons are murderers.
> 3. I created a murderer.

It is the same syllogism which produced all those mythic fathers who were convinced their sons would kill them. Being unable to see, accept and then deal with his or her violence, the parent transfers it in toto to the child by treating the child from the outset as a violent and dangerous creature who must be forcibly tamed.

To salve his spirit Victor sets out on a horse trip through the Alps, coming at last to Chamonix. On the glacier there, in a field of ice, father and son meet.

•

For many centuries men have been more or less consistently oppressive toward women, and women have more or less acquiesced in the oppression. During that time men spoke, they felt, for all humanity. So sure of their rightness were the English-speaking males that the word "man" came to mean all humanity while the word "woman" meant only half of humanity. In the past two hundred years women have begun to report on their view of the oppression, and to do something about it. Their view, stated through the actions and literature of the feminist move-ment as well as in the lives of many individual women, is somewhat at odds with the longstanding view which men have held of themselves as the only possible rulers of families, nations, and the planet.

Kate Millett pointed out some time ago that the power of the patriarchy rests on a three-cornered base consisting of women, children, and young males. Each of those three groups is exploited in different ways to provide support for the maintenance of the patriarchal structure. Women have for some time now been at work chang-ing the inequities to which they are subject in this system of things. The hippie rebellion represented the protest of a significant proportion of one generation of young males against their fathers' filicidal dominion. But what of the children?

How will we ever get the child's, the infant's version of what we have done to it? Perhaps it is impossible. Study of the self and observation of others yields clues. One can pierce the curtain of repression hanging over the past, up to a point. But what lies beyond that point? No infant can speak to us and communicate the reali-ty of its feelings in the first year or two of life when the act of filicide is usually carried out. And we have every reason to distrust our adult observations of parent-infant interaction. They are most likely as self-serving as the male-authored analyses of "femininity" and "woman's place," from St. Paul to Freud, so beloved of patri-archs past and present. The actual experience of filicide is securely hidden in all our minds, but those preliterate, preverbal memories are stored away in areas of the mind marked NON-EXISTENT at worst, or MYTHIC at best. We forget, and we forget we have forgotten.

As awareness of the magnitude of our oppression enters our consciousness and as our behavior toward our adult selves begins to change from control to love, our attitude toward other persons, including—mirabile dictu—children, also changes. Somewhere in the process perhaps some of us will attain sufficient sensitivity that we may capture in some medium the infant's response to filicide. Our presently rather badly atrophied sense of empathy may, as we begin to develop it consciously, yield a picture of the long-hidden universal experience of filicide.

Until that happens, one of the most extraordinary attempts at such a report is the one contained in this meeting between Victor and his son. Analyses of the most profound aspects of human experience using the scientific way of knowledge can, at this late date, be pretty well dismissed out-of-hand, because that way of knowledge is so thoroughly contaminated by filicidal limitations and motivations. Art is its own way of knowledge based on a paradoxical combination of control ("technique") and loss of control ("ecstasy," for want of a better term). The knowledge acquired through the process of art is often at odds with the knowledge acquired from the institutionalized ways of patriarchal knowledge. The ecstasy of the creative process places one outside one's normal, everyday self, and by a mysterious harmony one then functions as a medium through which ordinarily inaccessible knowledge and realities flow. It is of course the same process no matter what discipline one is working in, whether one calls it art, or religion, or even science. For some reason that behavior which we call art has resisted institutionalization better than have other behaviors, such as that which we call science. Perhaps we can therefore put somewhat greater trust in the reports of artists when we come to deal with the hidden realities of human behavior.

Art is also subject to self-serving error. What Shelley recorded as happening between father and son may be less than accurate. My experience as child and parent— to the extent that I am able to face honestly my behavior as parent and can remember my experience as child—and my observations of human behavior past and present indicate that she came very close to speaking the truth about what transpires between all parents and all children in this civilization, namely, filicide.

The meeting which she describes is between two males, and I shall discuss it in terms of masculine behavior, as father meets son. It would be erroneous and dangerous to assume that the same scene is not played out in only slightly different terms between mothers and daughters, with the same rejection, the same denial of love, the same competitiveness, the same acceptance of hatred as norm, the same psychological violence.

•

Two men meet on a glacier. If warmth is to come, it must come from them. They meet alone. For males this scene is the universe. It is all of life: the meeting with the ugly, threatening, hostile, deceitful, violent, murderous Other. Since we recognize no equals except creatures of our own species and gender, this meeting for a man is always with another male, who is always our father, our son, our self. Those other meetings—with women, with children, with young males, with the vast collection of objects we call nature—all those meetings are subordinate to this meeting of equals, this test of wills, this proof of manhood. The meeting occurs in two stages. In the first stage the participants determine which, if either, will blink first, which will back down first. If neither party blinks, the second stage follows immediately. This is the real battle for supremacy, to prove that one person is better at controlling than the other. In the second stage all restraint is dropped and each individual uses all the weapons he has been able to develop in his filicidal life. The second stage may consist of anything from a very subtle battle for psychological control to some form of the classic filicidal solution to major problems, physical violence.

When Victor first sees the monster running across the glacier he is terrified, but he recovers quickly.

> I trembled with rage and horror, resolving to wait his approach and then close with him in mortal combat. He approached; his countenance bespoke bitter anguish, combined with disdain and malignity, while its unearthly ugliness rendered it almost too horrible for human eyes. But I scarcely observed this; rage and hatred had at first deprived me of utterance, and I recovered only to overwhelm him with words expressive of furious detestation.

So the first thing Father does is to give Son a tongue-lashing:

> "Devil," I exclaimed, "do you dare approach me? And do you not fear the fierce vengeance of my arm wreaked on your miserable head? Begone. . .! Or rather, stay, that I may trample you to dust!"

Do you dare approach me, your creator? I, the unapproachable, the divinely untouchable, pronounce judgment on you, my son, and my judgment is that you are worthless. I reject you completely. I expose you on the mountainside, I cast you out of Paradise, I circumcise you, I crucify you, I curse you from the grave.

And how does the son respond to this outpouring of hatred from his father?

> "I expected this reception," said the demon. "All men hate the wretched; how, then, must I be hated, who am miserable beyond all living things! Yet you, my creator, detest and spurn me, thy creature, to whom thou art bound by ties dissoluble only by the annihilation of one of us. You purpose to kill me. How dare you sport thus with life? Do your duty towards me, and I will do mine towards you and the rest of mankind. If you will comply with my conditions, I will leave them and you at peace; but if you refuse, I will glut the maw of death, until it be satiated with the blood of your remaining friends."

Monster or not, this is no ordinary son. In contrast to his father's rage, his response is a model of patriarchal cool. He is not in the least intimidated by Victor's threats of physical violence. Neither does he laugh at the ridiculous spectacle that this person two feet smaller than he makes of himself. He reminds Victor of the actual nature of their relationship, for Victor appears not to realize that he is cast in the role of father to this unlikely creature-of-a-son. Being physically larger and more powerful than his father, this son can make demands and bargain in ways no human infant ever could. And he does so with a straightforward rationality any patriarch would have to admire. But for all his size and strength, he is still a child. He is dpendent on Victor and he knows it. *The problem is me and the solution is my father.*

Neither in this first meeting nor in any subsequent meeting does the son threaten his father directly with physical violence. Is it possible that our sons are not quite the patricidal maniacs which our own worst fears about ourselves and our adult capacity for violence lead us to believe? This monstrous son may articulate the infant's filicidal pain as none of us ever could, but even he fails to see that the problem originates with his father's behavior toward him, with his father's rejection of him as an independent entity responsible for his own behavior and development. Part of the filicidal deal is that both parent and child unquestioningly and unconsciously accept the validity of the filicidal syllogism. That being the case, the son does threaten persons close to Victor. Violence or the threat of violence is the accepted way to get Victor to do his duty (we will find our shortly just what Victor's duty is, as the son understands it). If Victor fails to do his duty, the son feels that his life will be meaningless and that he can do nothing but cause Victor maximum pain as Victor has caused him maximum pain.

As Shelley has the monster put it, we are bound by "ties dissoluble only by the annihilation of one of us." The reality of the human situation is that we are locked in mortal embrace. We share this universe, this planet, this existence, but the filicidal aspect of ourselves cannot tolerate the thought of any other entity trespassing on what we filicidally see as *my* universe. Transfigured by our filicidal fury, the human situation becomes one in which we are locked in mortal combat. The proto-scene becomes the model and source for that way of being which we call reality. In that scene our two basic choices—to love or to fight, embrace or combat—are reduced to one: we fight. And we want so desperately to fight to the death, to get rid of all those other no-good sons-of-fathers. . . but something has held us back as a race up to now from the total yielding up of ourselves to Thanatos. We can now state the theory of filicide in its simplest form: we want to destroy because we have been destroyed (or so we believe).

Freud, unable to see and accept his own filicide, at the end of his life was reduced to darkest pessimism as he finally had to face the Manichean orthodoxy which had been implicit in the theory of psychoanalysis from the beginning, namely the assumption that human beings and their cultures are trapped in a hopeless struggle between the forces of life (Eros) and the forces of death (Thanatos). That our seemingly instinctual commitment to the forces of death might spring from some culture-based experience escaped him.

We destroy because we have been destroyed. But somewhere, usually far beyond the limits of this defense mechanism personality we create in ourselves as a result of that destruction, there eixsts awareness and knowledge of potentials greater and finer than those expressed in our incessant, internecine battles. It is that knowledge which holds us back from the final war. Wanting to fight all the time, we find ourselves restrained, faced with an unending series of half-battles. Confronted with the incomprehensible fact that we cannot unleash our supposedly infinite filicidal prowess, we react like spoiled, angry children (since that is in essence what we are) and make the hourly, daily half-battles even deadlier and more intense. We fight to live and we live to fight.

There's more to our aggression yet. We are restrained not only by portions of ourselves which lie outside of our filicidal consciousness. We are also restrained by a paradoxical situation within our filicidal behavior. If the real fight to the death occurs and the enemy is eliminated, then who am I to fight? My filicidal life loses its meaning precisely to the extent that I am a genuinely successful filicidal adult. This I, this filicidal self, has been constructed, trained, and reared to control, but I have to be careful not to control too much because if I do there won't be anything left to control. If the son kills the father, if the monster kills Frankenstein, his life becomes meaningless. The monster knows that. The same holds for Frankenstein. If he kills his son, his life too becomes meaningless. What evidence do we have that, if he did kill the monster, he could return to Geneva, marry Elizabeth, and settle down to a life of contented contemplation of the beauties of his wife, his possible future children, and his old adversary nature? None. His whole life has been spent in the pursuit of control, with only brief rest and recreation breaks in which he catches his breath and enjoys a short dose of domestic tranquillity or natural beauty.

He, of course, thinks that the life of domestic repose is the one he wants. All of us compulsive workers and controllers who are existing at levels of affluence above subsistence are striving for the same end—the good life. It is the visionary rallying flag every ideology hoists over the distant and rather vague finish line. But even when we get old and in accordance with our social training convincingly pretend to ourselves and to others that the vital energies of life are almost exhausted and we "retire," even then notice how many of us have difficulty in making the adjustment to the good life of domestic tranquillity. If that is the case when we are old, are we to expect a man at the height of his powers (as we are so fond of putting it) to retire from the battlefield to a life of quietude, serenity, and repose? Or course not, at least not as long as that man does not understand what has been driving him to exist on and for that battlefield.

Victor responds to his son's calm and reasoned statement with another outburst of verbal abuse. His rage overcomes him and he hurls himself at the nameless creature. The father strikes the son. But this son easily eludes this father, physically anyway. And again the son speaks with quiet reason:

> *"Be calm! I entreat you to hear me before you give vent to your hatred on my devoted head. . . .* [He then points out that he is physically superior to Victor.] *But I will not be tempted to set myself in opposition to thee. I am thy creature, and I will be even mild and docile to my natural lord and king, if thou will also perform thy part, the which thou owest me. Oh, Frankenstein, be not equitable to every other and trample upon me alone, to whom thy justice, and even thy clemency and affection, is most due. Remember that I am thy creature; I ought to be thy Adam, but I am rather thy fallen angel, whom thou drivest from joy for no misdeed. Everywhere I see bliss, from which I alone am irrevocably excluded. I was benevolent and happy; misery made me a fiend. Make me happy, and I shall again be virtuous."*

The monstrous son asks the monstrous father for help, but it is already too late. The son is already molded by the filicidal stamp. He can seek salvation and redemption only outside of himself. He admits he is devoted to Victor, he acknowledges Victor as his "natural lord and king." But he does not understand. He blames his fall from goodness not on Victor but on humanity. It's their fault. And he is also already the dupe of the great grown-up deception. He has fallen for the front of happiness and bliss which humanity puts up before itself and its children. He has fallen for our pretense of successful control. The son obviously does not, cannot understand the world, but anyone wise enough to create him and bring him into the world must understand it. Therefore he throws himself on the mercy of the omniscient father: "Make me happy, and I shall again be virtuous."

Not only has the monster fallen for the appearance of happiness in humanity generally. He apparently has also been observing Victor's life, since in his opinion Victor behaves equitably toward everyone except him. Like the infant lying in the crib, the monster has had to view humanity from a distance, relying solely on his powers of observation. He can't get close enough to ask questions because everyone flees at the sight of him; He has observed adults, as we all did during infancy, and what he has observed is the surface of filicidal reality, that slick, convincing surface determined by the rules of filicidal behavior.

Everything appears to be well under control. He has watched, as we did, the skilled grown-up actors moving about in front of the artfully painted scenery-flat of reputation and respectability which we have erected to impress the neighbors, the boss, and other nations, and to convince ourselves that the roles we are playing are correct and justifiable. Like the Greek writers of tragedy, we find it most effective for all concerned if the really bloody action takes place offstage (except in times of direst emergency, such as war). Each of us even carries a piece of the scenery about with us in the form of clothes. We spend a great deal of time keeping the scenery clean and tidy and safe. Both the scenery and the acting are so convincing that we ourselves fail to notice the decay and flabbiness of the covered bodies and the turgid viscosity of the emotional morass in the societally concealed minds. All the rest, the real, smelly rot, is kept at a safe distance, well offstage, where we find that vast cultural landfill of humanity consisting of the poor, the insane, the criminal, the dying, and the already dead.

One might easily recast the entire theory of filicide in theatrical terminology. Were it not so deadly, we might see our behavior as the ultimate in method acting. As adults we are constantly playing to an audience, ignorant of the fact that we have a responsibility and a potential to live improvisationally in any way we can dream of. So caught up in the roles are we that we remain ignorant of the fact that the audience is also playing a role and that role interchange is constantly going on. We are now the actor, now the audience. As long as we succeed in the role, we are happy and can either ignore the mess backstage or blame it on someone else. We are such good actors by now that it is no wonder that the infant in the crib is taken in by our performance.

Or we might recast the theory in pedagogical, educational terms. The traditional classroom situation is only a somewhat formalized re-creation of the proto-scene. The experienced, certifiably educated adults have set the problems for the class. They, as the teachers, have determined which problems shall be dealt with. They have also determined what shall be considered the correct answers to those problems. They grade the tests and punish those who do poorly. And it's the only game in town, educationally.

So our monster throws himself on his omniscient teacher-creator and pleads, "Make me happy!" Too late. The son is already a filicide-in-training. His plea is phrased in terms of duty, debt, and obligation, the standard terms in which men deal with the world. We act from duty, not from love. Why? Because we act out of guilt. And where does the guilt come from? From the debt we owe our omniscient parents because of the bargain they struck with us by deigning to help and raise and train such ignorant and unworthy creatures as ourselves. It is the very bargain we see being struck here between this improbable father and his improbable son.

Again the story of Frankenstein brings us closer to the true nature of filicide. The mythological sons we looked at earlier never asked their fathers for anything. But here on the glacier the son asks the father for help, and—as we shall soon see—the father eventually agrees to the son's request. Reluctantly, but he does agree. What is at work here is one of the subtler mechanisms of filicide. The son is not yet wholly a creature of violence the way the father is, which means the son can still ask for love, in one form or another, as the monster does here. And the father says yes, all right, I'll give you what you want.

For clarity, let's get a bit ahead of the story. What the monster is working up to is that Victor create a mate for him. Victor will agree; and as Victor is working on the new female creature, the monster does become the virtuous person he had promised Victor he would be if Victor helped him. Then at the last minute, as Victor is about to animate the new woman, he has second thoughts and destroys her instead. It is that betrayal of the monster's trust which finally kills the son.

What is significant about the son's request for help is not only that he has fallen for the filicidal front of successful control, he has also unwittingly accepted the masculine view of woman as property. And the masculine view of woman as solution to the problems of masculine filicidal existence. That view of woman is another of the implicit promises which fathers make to sons as they raise them in the nuclear family. Obviously, mothers make a similar analogous promise to their daughters. There lies the schizoid essence of the traditional feminine role: men make women chattel and at the same time elevate them to such heights of expected goodness, gentleness, and loving affection that they come to be seen—and they come to see themselves—almost as redeeming angels.

In effect the monster says, "Father, give me a woman and I will be virtuous." As it happens, of course, Victor, the super-scientist, is in a position to grant this request. But the giving is an illusion. That is what Victor realizes just before he animates her. His second creation will have a mind of her own and may well react to the son with the same horror and rejection with which Victor and others have reacted to him. What then? Neither Victor nor the monster realizes what Shelley clearly knew, that the only thing either of them can give the other is the forgiveness of friendship and that the rest of whatever salvation it is our lot to know is up to the individual. For, having opened himself to friendship with all persons and things, male and female, animate and inanimate, the individual is on the way to being freed from the consuming forces of fear, guilt, hatred, and the need to control which comprise the syndrome called filicide. If Victor had been able to forgive himself for creating his son, and if his son had been able to forgive Victor for creating him as he is—ugly, monstrous, an object of universal loathing—then matters might have turned out differently. But that is the same as saying, if Jehovah had forgiven himself. So deep does our filicidal experience run and so long has it been running that such an act of self-forgiveness is almost unthinkable. We can hardly imagine the outcome if we were to change mortal combat to mortal embrace.

Back on the glacier, the father-son encounter continues in much the same style of attack and riposte. The monster has not yet revealed his request. All he asks of Victor for now is that Victor listen to his story of what has happened to him since he was "born." Victor, who still can't let go of his anger, blurts out the accusation that the monster murdered young William and, in effect, Justine. Victor's son may be a monster and a naive one at that but he's nobody's fool. He comes right back with:

> "The guilty are allowed, by human laws, bloody as they are, to speak in their own defense before they are condemned. Listen to me, Frankenstein. You accuse me of murder, and yet you would, with a satisfied conscience, destroy your own creature. Oh, praise the eternal justice of man!"

Not bad for a one-year-old. With his child's eyes he has seen through at least part of adult hypocrisy, that part in which we transfer the blame for our own violence and suffering to this or that person or group of persons whom we call "the enemy," so that we then feel little or no guilt about killing off those persons. To gain such illusorily cathartic satisfaction we have to ignore the metafamilial reality which lies just beneath the surface of this meeting between Frankenstein and his monster. Biologically they are not father and son. Legally they are not father and son. But the unique nature of their relationship forces them to behave according to the only model either of them has, the traditional microfamilial father-son model. Their situation at the same time forces them toward an awareness of their larger, metafamilial relationship for which neither they nor we have any very good models. They both resist accepting awareness of the fact that their most important relationship is their common membership in the family of humanity. It is only the desperate nature of the monster's situation that causes him to goad Frankenstein toward awareness that they are as much brothers as they are father and son.

Victor's response remains that of the orthodox older male. He is trapped in the father-role, and his fatherly conscience begins to bother him.

> For the first time, also, I felt what the duties of a creator towards his creature were, and that I ought to render him happy before I complained of his wickedness.

Victor finally agrees to hear the monster's story.

Which brings us to an unprecedented scene, one which has not been matched since.

The one-year-old infant has gotten Daddy's attention and has further persuaded him to sit down and listen to his story of what it's like to be cast out of Eden. Normally, when father meets son or mother meets daughter, it is not human meeting human but role meeting role. And because the parent, being so much bigger and older and more experienced, has all the marbles at the start, the child can never win, can never really play because the parent—together with the parent's culture—also dictates the rules. One of those rules is that creative play is out of the question. By the time the child gets some marbles of her own, she can play only by her parents' filicidal rules. Here Shelley has created for us a son who, though well on his way to becoming a committed and trapped player like the rest of us, is miraculously able to speak of his infant experience of filicide.

It is an intensely masculine scene, this meeting between Frankenstein and his monster. To get it into the larger human perspective, consider this: how would this scene and the novel be different if Victor had created a female instead of a male? Would we not have had a very similar confrontation, but with the female monster speaking charges which would sound very familiar to us? Would not her charges be essentially those which the feminist movement has brought against all us patriarchs together with our accessorial matriarchs-in-waiting? Having created a male, in other words having re-created himself, what Victor hears instead is a catalog of the crimes of himself against himself coming from this miracle monster-child who has the articulateness of an adult.

The monster's story of his first year of life—from the night of his birth when Victor fled to this meeting on the glacier—comprises the central section of the novel (Chapters 11-16). It is not often that we masculine masters of the earth get such a chance to see ourselves as the Other sees us. Shelley gives us an impossible report from an impossible creature—a one-year-old who feels, thinks, and talks.

•

The nameless son's earliest memories are vague. When he first opens his eyes on the night of his birth he sees only dim outlines, and his first attempts at movement are painful and clumsy. He is aware that he is alone, but he does not know that Victor has fled in terror. He takes some of Victor's clothes and stumbles into the darkness, winding up in a forest where he sleeps. The following day he comes across a fire in the forest. He burns himself, then figures out how to use dry wood to keep the fire going and discovers how to cook nuts. Several days pass during which he manages his survival quite well. It begins to snow and he seeks shelter in a village—his first encounter with people. The villagers are terrified. Some run from him, some attack him. He escapes easily.

After a period of aimless wandering he finds a shed attached to the back of an isolated cottage. This shed becomes his home for a year, the year of his infancy. The people in the cottage never use the shed. The monster hides there by day and goes out by night to find food. Through a chink in the wall of the cottage he has visual and audial access to the world of adult humanity as reflected in the family living there.

The situation Shelley has contrived here is that of the infant lying in its crib, observing adult human beings going about their business, slowly figuring out what that business is and how you do it. But this infant is deprived of the warmth of physical contact and affection. He watches and listens. Months pass as he learns the basic words. He is content. He is warm and secure and finds plenty to eat and drink.

In the gradually unfolded story of the inhabitants of the cottage—we learn their story at the same rate as the monster does—Shelley has created a small novel-within-a-novel. Again, as in her picture of Victor Frankenstein's idyllic childhood family, she here gives us—and the monster—a highly idealized view of a family. Three persons inhabit the cottage: an old man, who the monster eventually realizes is blind, a young man who works hard in the fields, and a young woman who cares for the house. Though they exist in poverty, the monster is struck by their openly displayed love for one another. They are never angry, they never complain, and they devote much time to entertaining and cheering each other up with songs and stories read aloud. Beneath this surface the monster perceives a deep sadness which he is at a loss to figure out. He wants to join them but is afraid to reveal himself. At night he has dreams of becoming a member of the family. During the day he has fantasies of being able to solve their problems for them and make them happy. His hopes of revealing himself to them suffer a severe setback one day when he accidentally sees his own image in a pond. The truth about himself begins to dawn: his appearance is a horrible parody of the human beauty of the cottagers.

Spring transforms the desolate landscape—it is the child's first spring—and the monster is overwhelmed by the experience. He becomes more and more hopeful, more and more eager to reveal himself.

Under mysterious circumstances a fourth person, a young woman, arrives one day and stays to live in the cottage. She does not speak the same language as the other three, though they obviously know her and are fond of her. They spend much time teaching her their language and reading aloud to her, which enables the monster to acquire something of an education. He hears three books read aloud: Plutarch's *Lives,* along with *The Sorrows of Young Werther,* and *Paradise Lost.* At night he steals into the cottage and borrows the books in order to teach himself to read. Obviously it is a rather patriarchal education that he is receiving (but then don't we all). As it progresses he becomes more and more aware of his predicament. There is no indication that there has ever existed a creature such as himself. He ponders his loneliness and begins to wonder about his origin. The plot creaks badly and he finds, in Victor's clothes which he had taken that first night, Victor's lab notes concerning his own creation. There he reads all the details concerning the origin of "my odious and loathsome person."

The monster stops his narrative and says to Victor:

> Why did you form a monster so hideous that even you turned from me in disgust? God, in pity, made man beautiful and alluring, after his own image; but my form is a filthy type of yours, more horrid even from the very resemblance. Satan had his companions, fellow devils, to admire and encourage him, but I am solitary and abhorred.

Hideous and filthy. Is the monster's ugliness only an externalization of the way Victor perceives himself internally (of, in other words, the way Mary Shelley perceived that men really see themselves)? Earlier in the novel Victor characterized his son as "my own spirit let loose from the grave and forced to destroy all that was dear to me." It seems this omnipotent creator has created his son in his own image: hideous and filthy. One is reminded of the complications arising from our own anatomy, with its fecal and urinary outlets so near the places of our greatest physical pleasure, the places of our own creation.

It is part of the acculturation package to learn that feces and urine are bad. We must then feel some sense of betrayal on the part of whatever larger force it is that as children we believe creates us. To think that this divine and divinely shaped form, that both I and you, beloved Caelia, shit. . .? Ah, such metaphysical treachery. Thus another part of our filicidal dissimulation is the pretense that we are clean and beautiful while we go around knowing that we are in places hideous and filthy and that we are in fact born from those places. We can hide the ugliness between our legs with clothes, but the ugliness of Frankenstein's monster extends over his whole body. Not only is he ugly, he is also alone:

> . . .no Eve soothed my sorrows nor shared my thoughts; I was alone. I remembered Adam's supplication to his Creator. But where was mine? He had abandoned me, and in the bitterness of my heart I cursed him.

The monster continues his story. Although he is despondent when he discovers the facts of his origin, he perseveres in his life adjacent to the cottagers. They seem much happier now that the fourth person has arrived. The monster sits for hours eavesdropping on their familial bliss.

The new arrival, Safie, is the only female character in the novel with some depth to her. As the monster pieces together her story from fragments of overheard conversations, one begins to suspect that we are hearing a fictionalized, romanticized version of Mary Shelley's own life. Reared in an "enlightened" household, Safie is very much on her way to being a liberated woman. Her mother was a "Christian Arab," originally a slave [!], who escaped her bondage and taught Safie "to aspire to higher powers of intellect and an independence of spirit." She describes her father as a man who, though brilliant and successful, was not above bartering his daughter's happiness in order to secure his own freedom in a situation which drove Safie to seek out the people in the cottage. We do not need to go further into the subplot which Shelley invents to bring these four people together. What is significant is the similarity between Safie's background and that of Shelley herself. Also significant is the fact that the character who most resembles Shelley appears inside the fourth frame of the novel.

Frame One is Walton writing Victor's story to his sister in England. Frame Two is Victor telling the story of his life to Walton. Frame Three is the monster telling his story to Victor. Frame Four is the monster overhearing Safie telling her story to the cottagers. There, tucked away in the innermost of these frames, Shelley gives us herself, or a part of herself.

For all her extraordinary ability, apparently Shelley was having some difficulty facing herself—a fact which is hardly surprising when one considers the intensely patriarchal figures surrounding her. Her father, William Godwin, was your classic liberal, in all senses of the word. For a husband, she had one of the great poetic talents of the age. And then there was her husband's close friend, Byron, he of the—dare I mention it—club foot.

As if those three men were not enough, she also had to contend with the accomplishments of her mother, Mary Wollstonecraft Godwin, the first modern woman to speak out clearly against man's inhumanity to woman and for woman's basic humanity. Her mother had died when Mary was born. Perhaps such diverse and powerful pressures were necessary for the creation of the patriarchal portrait she produced in *Frankenstein*. The fact that she inserts a picture of herself in the novel in such a guarded way gives some indication of the extent to which she had been unable to reconcile herself and her circumstances. Further evidence will be forthcoming shortly concerning the strength of the inner conflict which caused her to write such a work at the age of nineteen.

The monster finally decides to reveal himself to the family in the cottage. His plan is to make friends with the blind man when the other three are absent. He will win the old man's affection and then be able to describe to him his own ugliness. The old man will tell the others about his new friend and the monster can show himself to them with less fear of rejection.

One afternoon the three younger people leave the house and the monster makes his first contact with humanity as a thinking and speaking person. His conversation with the old man has hardly begun when the other three return unexpectedly. The monster suffers another instant rejection as the two women faint and the young man attacks him physically. Again he does not fight back but runs away into the forest; He says he became a "wild beast," howling his pain and anger to the unhearing trees and the singing birds:

> *"All, save I, were at rest, or in enjoyment; I, like the arch-fiend, bore a hell within me, and finding myself unsympathized with, wished to tear up the trees, spread havoc and destruction around me, and then to have sat down and enjoyed the ruin. . . . There was none among the myriads of men that existed who would pity or assist me; and should I feel kindness towards my enemies? No; from that moment I declared everlasting war against the species, and more than all, against him who had formed me and sent me forth to this insupportable misery."*

His filicide is nearly complete. His only pleasure is paiñ. Life has meaning only to the extent that he can fight against the species of man, and especially against his father. Since his filicide is not yet quite complete, he still has some hope. He tells Victor that he realized that "from you only could I hope for succor." All that is left in other words to make the monster a man is for him to suffer his father's ultimate rejection and betrayal.

Using a stolen map and traveling by night, he makes his way to Geneva. En route he has another humanizing experience. He saves a woman from drowning only to be shot at and wounded by the woman's husband. At that point, he says,

> *"All joy was but a mockery which insulted my desolate state and made me fail more painfully that I was not made for pleasure."*

Arriving in Geneva he conceals himself in a park, where he sleeps. He is awakened by the sound of a child at play. The idea occurs to him that the child, naive and innocent, might not react to him as adults do. But the child—it is of course William, Victor's young brother—reacts with terror and screams for help. Among the names he screams is his brother's. The monster makes the connection instantly and attacks and strangles the child.

As he runs away he encounters Justine who is napping nearby. Looking at her he comes as close to sex as nineteenth century convention would allow. From Shelley's veiled allusions it is clear the monster's sex is being stirred by the sight of the sleeping woman. He knows he can never know such a person:

> *I was forever deprived of the delights that such beautiful creatures*
> *could bestow. . . She. . . would, in regarding me, have changed that*
> *air of divine benignity to one expressive of disgust and affright.*

Faced with the choice now familiar to him—he can attempt love with a high probability of rejection or he can attempt destruction with a high probability of success—he chooses destruction and plants a locket on Justine which he had torn from
William's neck.

> *The sleeper stirred; a thrill of terror ran through me. Should she in-*
> *need awake, and see me, and curse me, and denounce the murderer?*
> *Thus would she assuredly act if her darkened eyes opened and she be-*
> *held me. The thought was madness; it stirred the fiend within me—not*
> *I, but she, shall suffer; the murder I have committed because I am for-*
> *ever robbed of all that she could give me, she shall atone. The crime*
> *had its source in her; be hers the punishment.*

In the middle of a nineteenth century horror story we find one of the clearest
imaginable statements of the ancient patriarchal rationale for misogyny. If this
monster is more new Adam than new Prometheus, then in this scene Justine plays
the new Eve and receives the full burden of Adam's filicidal anger resulting from
his father's rejection of him. Notice that Eve's role here is totally passive. She
doesn't have to do anything, not even pick an apple, to become the repository of
male guilt. Her very existence is reason enough, for she represents all that Adam can
no longer be because of his consuming fear, hatred, and anger—namely, tender, loving,
gentle, and beautiful. He will not let her control—and hurt—him by giving her the
chance to reject him. Rather, he will control her in the only way he knows how to
control, by destroying her, by making her appear guilty for William's death—just
as we attempted to control woman by making Eve appear to be the guilty party
for the alleged fall of *man*.

Since the murder, the monster says, he has been spying on the Frankenstein family
and living on the glacier. As he finishes the story of the first year of his life he
makes his request:

> *I am alone and miserable; man will not associate with me; but one as*
> *deformed and horrible as myself would not deny herself to me. My*
> *companion must be of the same species and have the same defects.*
> *This being you must create.*

This son without a name is indeed the miraculously speaking human infant. He, like
the infant, is totally dependent on his parent for his happiness and must beg the
parent for help. By the time we human children are old enough to talk, our filici-

dal acculturation has already progressed to the point where we cannot ask so directly as the monster does here for that which we really want, namely, love. But this
monster-child knows and states his need directly, without resorting to the endless
subterfuges of aging human children.

Victor's first response to the story and the request is anger, and he delivers himself
of a few more patriarchal "begone's" before he begins to soften. The monster
summarizes his case, promising that he will be a different person when he has a
mate and that he will live in some remote area with her and no longer be a threat to
humanity. He says:

> My vices are the children of forced solitude that I abhor, and my virtues
> will necessarily arise when I live in communion with an equal. I shall
> feel the affections of a sensitive being and become linked to the chain
> of existence and events from which I am now excluded.

The primary somatic effect of cultural filicide on males is that condition to which
the monster refers here. One is cut off from the "chain of existence," one no longer
feels organic or organismic ties to the world one inhabits. To use the twentieth
century term: one becomes alienated. Implicit in the monster's inference of his
alienation from the larger world is his alienation from himself, both from his
"hideous and filthy" body and from the better side of his psyche. He knows he is
not yet a creature of destruction, and he is desperately looking for a way to develop
the better side of himself. Since California was not yet available, he has no choice
but to ask his father for a mate. "My virtues will necessarily arise when I live in
communion with an equal," he says. He also knows there is a limit to the amount
of rejection he can experience and still retain a belief in his own goodness.

Presented with this reasoned argument, Victor yields and agrees to construct a mate
for him. He still has serious doubts about the wisidom of the undertaking and resorts to the classic filicidal justification for doing something of a highly dubious
nature. He will do it not for himself but for his family:

> . . .to save them, I resolved to dedicate myself to my most abhorred
> task. The prospect of such an occupation made every other circum-
> stance of existence pass before me like a dream, and that thought only
> had to me the reality of life.

Once again he is in the grip of a compulsion, and once again all aspects of life become unreal to him except his work—and the thought that he is doing this to save
his family. The monster is not the only alienated person in the story. Victor com-
ments on the "insurmountable barrier between me and my fellow men" which the
project erects.

Following a brief, happy interlude in Geneva, during which he and Elizabeth decide to marry as soon as his work is finished (he of course does not tell her the nature of his new project), he goes to a remote part of Scotland, sets up a laboratory, and begins the creation of a woman, a daughter. His self-hatred knows almost no bounds as he assembles this second creature:

> *I was formed for peaceful happiness. During my youthful days discontent never visited my mind, and if I was ever overcome by ennui, the sight of what is beautiful in nature or the study of what is excellent and sublime in the productions of man could always interest my heart and communicate elasticity to my spirits. But I am a blasted tree; the bolt has entered my soul; and I felt then that I should survive to exhibit what I shall soon cease to be—a miserable spectacle of wrecked humanity, pitiable to others and intolerable to myself. . . . I felt as if I had committed some great crime, the consciousness of which haunted me. I was guiltless, but I had indeed drawn down a horrible curse upon my head, as mortal as that of crime.*

How like his son he sounds. If the monster is an aging child, then Victor is an aging monster. But his only crime is that of filicide. In fact, he is in a sense guilty of double filicide, because he has created a sort of double monster. First, he created his son in the shape of a physical monster—our own sons and daughters have to experience years of acculturation before becoming convinced of the ugliness of their bodies. Second, he has committed traditional cultural filicide by failing from the start to deal with his son as an independent entity. By failing to love his son, he has created a psychological monster. As in all his dealings with his son, so too with this attempt to help him: he goes about it not out of a sense of joy, a sense of being able to help another being get on with the business of living, but out of a sense of burdensome duty:

> *. . . now I went to it in cold blood, and my heart sickened at the work of my hands.*

He senses that the monster has followed him to Scotland and is secretly watching to make sure he keeps his side of the bargain. After several months of work the moment is at hand to animate the woman. Victor suddenly has second thoughts. Can he trust the monster to keep his word? What if the woman is as repulsed by the sight of her proposed mate as the rest of humanity is? What will the woman think of herself? She will be an independent creature and in no way bound to keep a promise made on her behalf before she was born. Victor's train of thought carries him rapidly to another of the classic patriarchal justifications for the really big decisions which one must occasionally make: what will the judgment of history be?

> *I shuddered to think that future ages might curse me as their pest,*
> *whose selfishness had not hesitated to buy its own peace at the price,*
> *perhaps, of the existence of the whole human race.*

Nowadays our filicidal rationalizations are a bit more refined, so that we can convince ourselves that history will judge peace through carpet bombing as laudable and exemplary behavior. For nineteenth century Victor, this thought about the judgment of history is what brings the project to a halt. He looks up from his work table and sees the monster looking in the window. Victor hurls himself at the lifeless woman and tears the body apart. He hears the monster scream and run away.

The filicide is complete. By destroying the daughter, Victor has destroyed the son. It is a deed and a scene almost too rich in Oedipal as well as filicidal overtones and echoes upon echoes of frustrated love and broken trust from our long familial tradition. How are we to read this remarkable scene? Do we see here Shelley's hatred of her own female self coming to the surface? Or is it a reflection of her awareness of the rampant, pathological hatred of women in this civilization? Is it the hatred of her mother whom she perhaps felt she could not equal? Or is it a reflection of her awareness of the Oedipal confusions and violence hidden in the hearts of men?

Or is it the final and most awful of the insights into the nature of filicidal reality? Namely, the realization that the only way the father can succeed in his patriarchal filicide is if he has already in effect killed the mother, and the realization that even the mother's attempts at love, however tainted, are themselves subject ultimately to the father's absolute and lethal control. If so, then in this patriarchy, the filicidal cry is not—as we had it before:

> *Father and Mother, how can you both do this to me?*

The filicidal cry is:

> *Mother, how can you let him do this to me?*

To which there is no answer. And somewhere, somehow we hide away the realization that woman is as much a victim of filicide as man.

It is the way Shelley relishes this scene, dwelling on naturalistic, almost gory detail—as she does in no other scene in the novel—which causes me to perceive dark and ancient resonances here from the universal screams of pain as the filicidal deed has been done and done again:

*The next morning, at daybreak, I summoned sufficient courage and un-
locked the door of my laboratory. The remains of the half-finished
creature, whom I had destroyed, lay scattered on the floor, and I almost
felt as if I had mangled the flesh of a human being. . . With trembling
hand I conveyed the instruments out of the room, but I reflected that
I ought not to leave the relics of my work to excite the horror and
suspicion of the peasants; and I accordingly put them into a basket,
with a great quantity of stones, and laying them up, determined to
throw them into the sea that very night; and in the meantime I sat upon
the beach, employed in cleaning and arranging my chemical appara-
tus. . . .*

*Between two and three in the morning the moon rose; and I then, put-
ting my basket aboard a little skiff, sailed out about four miles from the
shore. The scene was perfectly solitary; a few boats were returning
towards land, but I sailed away from them. I felt as if I was about the
commission of a dreadful crime and avoided with shuddering anxiety
any encounter with my fellow creatures. At one time the moon, which
before had been clear, was suddenly overspread by a thick cloud, and I
took advantage of the moment of darkness and cast my basket into the
sea. I listened to the gurgling sound as it sank, then sailed away from
the spot.*

With excitement and enthusiasm Frankenstein created his man. With fear and loathing he created his woman. If cultural filicide is the hidden atrocity in all our pasts,
whether we are male or female, perhaps matricide is the hidden desire behind the
lives of all men in this patriarchy. We create male lives and a male civilization in
which the opposite is manifested as an ideal: the sanctification of Mother. Perhaps
our patriarchal myths are intended not only to protect fathers against the knowledge of their own filicide but also to protect them (us) from the knowledge of
matricidal desires. Surely our anger with and disappointment toward our mothers,
who physically bore us and bore us into this world, must be very great. Perhaps it
is great enough when combined with our knowledge of their passive complicity in
the fathers' filicide, to cause us in total unconsciousness of what we are doing to
carry out matricidal vengeance on the women called our wives who are also our
mothers and our daughters. We never scream the filicidal scream:

Mother, how could you let him do this to me?

but the pain is always there and our vengeance is, in the planet-wide system of
feminine servitude, effectively matricide. Analogously, women, in addition to their
universal experience of filicide which they share with us, must live with the secret
feminine desire for patricide, for that vengeance which they could not carry out on

103

their fathers, on their husbands—who are also their fathers who are also their sons.

This confusion of powerful motivations makes somewhat clearer how it is that each generation of fathers and mothers so easily and readily ships off each generation of sons to martial slavery and daughters to marital slavery. Bringing together all this tangle of hate-filled behavior, both masculine and feminine, is the abundant and manifest self-hatred of Mary Shelley which finally comes gurgling to the surface in this scene, like so many fetid air bubbles rising from the pieces of decaying and very ancient female, human flesh at the bottom of the ocean of history.

Oedipal, Electral, filicidal, whatever label we put on the analysis of the politics of the family, it comes down to the same thing: necrophilia. Corpses fighting corpses for the control of other corpses. Why? Now, because it is habit. And tradition. And because we like it—we have come to prefer pain to pleasure, suffering to joy. Death to life. The compulsive pursuit of control at first brings security, which soon becomes stasis, which soon becomes paralysis, which then becomes that ongoing way of death we call history.

•

With this climactic scene, father and son have exhausted their options. All that is left for them now is mutual physical destruction. As Victor is cleaning the lab, the monster returns and they have their last conversation. It is brief. The son swears to strike back at Victor as Victor has struck at him. He says he will have his revenge on Victor's wedding night. Victor interprets this as a threat on his own life. His adoration of Elizabeth is so great that he cannot conceive that anyone might want to harm her.

Victor returns to Switzerland and suffers another extended breakdown. When he recovers he and Elizabeth are married in Geneva and go to Lake Como for their honeymoon. Victor leaves Elizabeth in the bridal suite. He is certain the monster is nearby. He takes his pistol to search out and slay the demon. His search is interrupted by Elizabeth's dying screams as the monster kills her.

The father destroys the son-brother-father's life. The son destroys the father-brother-son's life. In this endless canon of patriarchal filicide, women function again and again as surrogate victims. As men have spread their stifling cloak of masculine violence over the planet, they may have physically killed more men than women in the bloody ritual of control known as war. Along the way men may also have killed themselves psychologically by entrapping each new generation of sons in the vicious circle which teaches that control is the only way to live and violence is the only way to control. Beyond those physical and psychological deaths are the raped and murdered women who have fallen victim to their own passive complicity as each generation of sons took their vengeance on the daughters for what their mothers allowed their fathers to do to them. It is truly a behavioral knot whose tangles within tangles are worthy of five thousand years of history and five billion human lives.

In *Frankenstein* Shelley created a precise summary of the course of history, reduced to the four basic characters: father, son, mother, daughter. Just as Victor is really no father at all, Elizabeth is no mother. Neither of their bodies is needed for the creation of their son or their daughter. The son is such a monster that he lives only with great difficulty. The daughter does not live at all. Must we not read in this the most damning judgment of all against men as masters of this civilization? However tragic and bloody the lives of men may be, they at least have a slim chance to explore their human potential. Women, Shelley is telling us here, are still-born in this culture, so deadly and swift and total is their filicidal acculturation.

•

We are back to Frame One. Victor, on the ship in the Arctic Ocean, brings his story to Walton to a quick conclusion. He has been pursuing the monster all over the world. The monster toys with him, leaving clues here and there, letting Victor catch an occasional glimpse of him, sometimes backtracking and pretending that it is he who is pursuing Victor. Now the monster has led him to this world of ice. Old and weakened by exposure to the harsh climate, Victor is near death. He tells Walton that in the last months of the chase he feels he has been freed from the hatred which had driven him so long. At night, he says, he finds solace in a continuing series of beautiful dreams which he believes are harbingers of a life after death. Victor's last words are:

> *Seek happiness in tranquillity and avoid ambition, even if it be only the apparently innocent one of distinguishing yourself in science and discoveries. Yet why do I say this? I myself have been blasted in these hopes, yet another may succeed.*

A few hours later Walton hears sounds coming from the cabin where Victor's body lies. He approaches and sees the monster standing over the corpse making "exclamations of grief and terror." Walton is suitably horrified by the monster's appearance but he had promised Victor that if the monster came he would in some way deal with him. Frankenstein's son has one last meeting with humanity in which he describes to Walton his version of the years since Victor destroyed his mate. He says that following his murder of Elizabeth he felt nothing:

> *I had cast off all feeling, subdued all anguish, to riot in the excess of my despair. Evil henceforth became my good. . . . I cannot believe*

105

that I am the same creature whose thoughts were once filled with sub-
lime and transcendent visions of the beauty and majesty of goodness.
But it is even so; the fallen angel becomes a malignant devil. Yet even
that enemy of God and man had friends and associates in his desola-
tion. I am alone.

The complete filicide. A mythic creature whose filicidal perfection has perhaps been approached only by the most extreme tyrants and murderers. He cannot feel. He is alone in a world without warmth. Living, he is dead. He is us and he is not us. He is us to the extent that we all behave, though less intensely and consistently, in the ways we have seen so intensely and consistently displayed by this mythic father and son. He is not us in the sense that this living death is only the way we think we have to be and not, in fact, the way we have to be. Our cultural filicidal view of ourselves is in its way as much a fiction as is Shelley's depiction of us—the difference being that we have made art life, while Shelley made life art.

Frankenstein ends in death, in a world of ice. The monster leaves Walton, telling him he is going to commit suicide. He plans to build a fire using wood from his sled and throw himself onto it. The creature who never knew the warmth of a human embrace, not even the warmth of the womb, the creature who never existed but who exists in us all, dies still seeking warmth. Our last glimpse of the name-less son comes as we see him wandering off alone across an endless sea of ice toward his self-contrived death.

In a very real sense the novel is profoundly prophetic. Shelley shows us ourselves, filicidal and death-centered as we are. The disease called man. But more elegantly understood than with Nietzsche, and more compassionately depicted than with Freud. Her prophecy is simple: death-centered behavior produces death. Tem-porizing measures such as gun control laws, nuclear arms agreements, ecumenical accords, clean air acts, are good. But as long as we remain within the smothering confines of traditional historical roles, such measures do little more than postpone the filicidal armageddon.

At the same time that America has experimented with the encouragement of freedom on a vaster scale than has any civilization before us, we have continued to be brutal and vicious, oppressive and violent on repeated occasions at home and abroad. The distance between American ideals and American reality has been as much a puzzle to us as a delight to our enemies. Time and again we have been brought up short, left standing in confused and bloody consternation, as the creative solutions freedom nurtures have been repeatedly mocked and shattered by our violence in times of crisis. An understanding of filicide offers some help in analyzing the difficulty we have had in utilizing our freedom in positive ways. The conclusion cannot be avoided that the yin of American freedom is balanced rather neatly by the yang of American filicide. If control is the primary form of filicidal behavior, then America must represent the fullest flowering of filicidal culture. Our skill at controlling is such that the English verb "manage" has made its way into any number of languages.

And we have managed very well indeed. The moon flights were awesome in their complex, cold perfection. Presidential elections have become a series of minor masterpieces of conscious, calculating manipulation of the entire country. But even as we achieved near-perfect control in many areas, collapse had already begun—at the hands of a nation hardly a twentieth our size. For reasons which baffled us all, but especially our trigger happy leaders, we could not bring ourselves to unleash our strength even for the few minutes necessary to destroy the pesky, feisty enemy. We failed to be classically victorious in Vietnam because we were getting very near the point of no return in the filicidal script.

The filicidal mask of control, even as such seeming opposites as Neil Armstrong and Richard Nixon were putting the finishing touches on it, was cracking. We reached a point where we saw that to persist, to force life to exist inside that hollow, lifeless face meant that we had to be prepared to watch ourselves kill our children openly and without pretense. We tested pure, undisguised filicide at Jackson State and at Kent State. We recoiled. We walked right up to the edge of the abyss of child-murder—which is of course always self-murder, the same brink over which so many well-intentioned societies have plunged before us, we walked to the edge of unrestrained tyranny, dropped a few of our children into the abyss, and backed

107

off. "No," we said. "Not that." We had finally found a price for classic, historical success that was higher than we were willing to pay.

What happens if Oedipus doesn't claw his eyes out, if Orestes doesn't kill his mother, if Agamemnon refuses to sacrifice Iphigenia, if God doesn't throw Adam and Eve out of Eden, if Abraham refuses to sacrifice Isaac, if we and God never send Jesus to the cross, if Hamlet refuses to be his father's avenger, if Frankenstein gives his son a hug? What happens if a nation with a long history of filicidal behavior and a long tradition of judging success by the competitive standard where victory = good and defeat = bad—what happens if such a nation refuses to win a simple little war against a hopelessly out-classed small nation?

One thing that happens is that voices of doom are heard in great humber, and they are right in their apocalyptic warnings—though not in the way they think. We were in Vietnam because we are not only our fathers' sons, we are also still trying to be our fathers. We got out of Vietnam because we somehow realized that if we won, we would lose. We realized that the only way to win was to lose. In the middle of a very bloody little war during which we had repeatedly made our fathers' old choice of mortal combat, we slowly changed our national mind and took the first step toward choosing mortal embrace by putting down our weapons and walking away. That it was an epochal gesture of breath-taking courage and beauty is a fact we are obviously having a hard time in recognizing. The warnings of the patriarchal prophets of doom are correct because that choice, if we continue to make it, does mean—just as they fear—the end to civilization as they know it.

The planetary bomb is still loaded, with a hair trigger. Many other steps of a similar kind have to be taken by many nations before the bomb is defused. Our own confused behavior in America since the Vietnam War shows that we are far from having irrevocably decided on the path of mortal embrace.

Since America is still a society in process, it is difficult to isolate our central myths. Given the nature of our first two centuries, we can safely settle on two myths for the purposes of discussion. One we might call the Wyatt Earp myth, the other, the Horatio Alger myth—the American versions of tragic failure, and tragic success. The Wyatt Earp myth arises from the need in a frontier society to establish law and order as quickly as possible and to maintain it with a minimum of disruption to the process of building a life in a wilderness. The Horatio Alger myth arises from a society which applies standards of cautious, violent control and hard-working vigilence as the only means of achieving security and peace in a frontier setting.

The experience of the frontier produced an American variation on classic, European filicide. Somehow, at the same time that we carted the old filicidal baggage across the ocean more or less intact, we left the fathers behind in Europe. On the vast, new continent we have been rather like children left alone in the nursery to fight it out among ourselves. Thus America has developed a filicidal civilization with a distinct fratricidal quality about it.

To be sure, we were aware of the grand European tradition of filicidal patriarchy. We have continuously toyed with overt father worship—as when, for example, we now and then elect a quasi-fascist president. On a less institutionalized basis we have toyed with mother worship. Just as the intense father religion of the Jews produced the intense son religion of the Christians, the intense father civilization of Europe produced the intense son civilization of America. Filicidal Christianity has as its central symbol the dead son on a cross. Fratricidal America has as its central symbol the shoot-out on Main Street. For America it is all the same myth that is acted out, whether the battle is between Wyatt Earp and Billy the Kid, between Lee Harvey Oswald and John Kennedy, between Martin Luther King, Jr. and James Earl Ray, between Lyndon Johnson and Ho Chi Minh, between National Guardsmen and Kent State students, between state policemen and Jackson State students.

Cain and Abel. Daddy is off at work somewhere. Mommy is at home. And there's nobody here but us kids to try and figure out what to do. Orwell spoke more strongly to America than to Europe because his terminology ("Big Brother") and vision were more closely in tune with the realities of this fratricidal version of filicidal civilization.

Extreme, bloody, emasculating racism of the sort America has displayed is possible only in a filicidal fratriarchy. In a smoothly functioning filicidal patriarchy harsh judgment is spread more or less equally among all citizens (except those of the ruling class). Street gangs provide an accurate reflection of basic American reality: tribes of boys fighting it out, with the girls standing on the sidelines shouting encouragement.

Football replaces baseball as the national sport because it is a more nearly overt acting out of the shoot-out myth. The field and the action are linear, like Main Street, and the object of the game is to get the other group's territory by physically defeating them. Baseball, however attractive its phallic symbolism, is played in a circular area where the struggle is based more on a shared agreement as to the use of the area. Baseball is also almost wholly lacking in the element of violent body contact. Violent touching appears to be more satisfying than not touching at all.

HORATIO ALGER

Success is so obviously a primary American value that to discuss it at this late date is to belabor the obvious. What is less apparent is the filicidal irony that undercuts our Orestes-like success. The irony is a dual one, part of which is geographic and part of which is sexual.

In our near-fatal immersion in materialistic values, we have measured success in terms of money and power. The great American fortunes are—so the myth goes—the result of hard work, clear thinking, and good planning. American geography adds an irony to such acquisitiveness which is lacking in Europe. We came to a virgin continent whose natural resources had hardly been touched by its ancient inhabitants. For a group of people with a compulsion to strive for material success, the continent was an enormous El Dorado, an untouched treasure house of immense size. Given the richness of the continent, it would be difficult for any kind of society to exist here long and not generate hundreds, thousands of amazing success stories. We have behaved like children wandering through a field littered with gold nuggets. Any child who stumbles across a nugget becomes the center of our attention, and that child's life and words take on great importance for us. We have naively and pridefully tended to ignore the simple fact that our success here is in large part due to the incredible bounty of nature which the new homeland offered. Part of the irony of our success is at last catching up with us as we slowly come to realize the environmental price we have to pay for our violent exploitation of those riches.

Horatio Alger was our only author able to successfully create an entire corpus of work centered around the myth of American success, though generally his models were oriented to a more urban, second-generation exploitation of wealth. Other writers have depicted the success myth in less stereotyped, more profound ways. But Alger was so accurate in his reproduction of the American ideal of success—that glittering surface we still want so much to believe is real and accessible to anyone who will just work hard enough—that his name became synonymous with the myth itself. His stories are so familiar to us that we don't even have to read them anymore. But his name and his life conceal the other half of the irony of American success: Horatio Alger was homosexual.

The geographic irony of American success lies in the fact that we have applauded and praised and memorialized ourselves for being such skilled controllers of the continent, and now it turns our that we who thought of ourselves as such great lovers have been little more than clumsy rapists. The sexual irony of American success lies in the fact that we have applauded and praised and memorialized ourselves for being such skilled and deft Men—manly, no-nonsense, brave, macho Daddys, and it turns out that all this time the American fratriarchy has been homoerotic.

The little boys in the nursery are very frightened of the little girls, but they can overpower the little girls because the boys are bigger and stronger. But the little boys are also frightened of each other. They know the terrible self-hatred and violence that resides in themselves is also found in their compatriots. Love is possible in a filicidal society between only those persons who can agree implicitly to relate in a filicidal way—which means violently. Since the little girls are—or appear to be—incapable of the level of violence of which the little boys are capable, the little boys are drawn irresistibly toward, and fascinated by, one another.

A major part of proving one's identity as a real father-son, a real man, consists in being a successful fucker of women. The fucking of men is taboo—except where it is done violently and harshly under extreme circumstances, as in prisons and armies. So the little boys compulsively copulate with the little girls and simultaneously sublimate their lethal fascination for each other by competing, by proving who has the larger and therefore better penis/body/mind.

Humans are violent to the extent that they cannot be loving. Men shoot other men because they cannot touch other men gently and lovingly. The American fratriarchy denies almost completely the possibility of genuine love between American men. Again we see that the fundamental attitude beneath our filicidal posturing—which in America has achieved a surface appearance of unprecedented attractiveness—is self-hatred.

As a young man Horatio Alger was a cleric in a small New England town. The pattern of his peaceful, pastoral life seemed set—until he was one day caught fooling around with the choirboys and immediately removed from his position. Lacking funds and with no immediate opportunity to earn funds, he went to New York and started writing stories about little boys who work hard and grow up to be successful big boys. The stories quickly found a wide, hungry audience. Horatio Alger became rich and famous. Horatio Alger's life is a Horatio Alger story.

Leslie Fiedler was the first to perceive the powerful undercurrent of homoeroticism in American literature. (The definitive analysis of homoeroticism in American culture is yet to appear.) The reader unfamiliar with Fiedler's work would do well to look into his eye-opening explication of, for example, *Huckleberry Finn.* Many other areas of the culture are filled with equally rich homoerotic ambiguity: the Hollywood Western (as Pat Dowell, the film critic, has noted), advertising, sports, etc.

The extent of the repression of our homoeroticism may be easily gauged by the intensity of American homophobia. From inane jokes to inane laws, American civilization seeks to deny its own reality. Filicidally, the dynamic of American homophobia may be understood in the following way. No matter how far away our fathers are—whether we left them behind culturally in Europe or whether they are just off at work most of the time—they still exist and their rejection of us is still real and painful, which means that our fear of them is also very great. The homosexual, as perceived by the so-called normal heterosexual male, seems to be mocking the normal male's greatest fear, that of his father. The homosexual male is known to love and have sex with other males. That sort of behavior is inadmissible in a filicidal, fratriarchal society because males are supposed to fight each other, not love each other. A person who mocks, or who seems to mock, our greatest fears, becomes the object of great fear himself, usually expressed in the form of anger and hate—hence the vehemence of American homophobia.

Another indication of the filicidal intensity of American civilization is the almost universal practice of circumcision. In the 1940s two large-scale studies of infant circumcision were conducted, one in Great Britain and one in the United States. The two studies came to opposite conclusions. In Great Britain it was found that infant mortality increased when circumcision was performed at, or soon after, birth. British doctors therefore ceased recommending it as a normal procedure. In the United States it was found that infant mortality decreased when circumcision was performed at, or soon after, birth. American doctors therefore began recommending it to their prenatal patients. In America it is ostensibly performed for hygienic reasons. The doctor will tell the parent who presses for information that it eliminates the necessity for cleaning the smegma from beneath the infant's foreskin. American parents have accepted the operation to such an extent that the percentage of American males who are circumcized is in the high nineties.

There are several strange aspects to the operation. For one, of course, it is a simple operation and an easy way for the physician to make a little extra money. Another puzzling aspect is the easy complicity of the mother, the readiness with which the mother accedes to the cutting of her baby. How easily we let ourselves believe (as did Laius and Jocasta) that the infant does not know what is happening to it, that the infant cannot feel pain. And notice that our scientific reason for the operation is to give our sons a greater chance to live. So, in examining our modern behavior we come full circle. We are back with Abraham and Isaac and all the other fathers saying to their sons as they raise the literal or psychological knife of filicide: *I'm doing this for your own good, my child.* Snip.

FASCISM AND FILICIDE

Fathers have taken several hards licks in this exposition of the theory of filicide. One of the major historical developments of the twentieth century, fascism, offers an opportunity to balance the books. *Frankenstein* revealed the precarious interplay between the basic needs of our survival and our filicidal need to control absolutely. If we control too well and too much we wind up with nothing left to control. Much of the thoughtful caution so frequently apparent in all levels of patriarchal planning (in the family, in business, in government) comes from an unconsciousness awareness of that fact.

Our patriarchal leaders take pride in the alleged wisdom of their thoughtfulness and prudence. Given our tendency toward violent solutions of maximum extremity, there may be something of real wisdom in our leaders' foot-dragging. If nothing else, we thereby buy time for ourselves. It is of course quite possible that we will use that time to develop bigger and better means of violent control rather than using it to examine and change our behavior. The point is, the successful filicide knows the value of restraint and learns to practice it with skill.

In this century humanity was faced with the astounding sight of three societies whose leaders blew the filicidal cover of restraint. Fascism is nothing more than filicide practiced on a national scale—without dissimulation. Apart from our human outrage at the brutal atrocities committed by the fascist nations, our reaction to fascism was so intense because—as filicidal patriarchs—we were apalled to see whole nations of filicidal patriarchs doing what we do but being honest about it. In Germany, Italy, and Japan, racist, sexist, elitist policies were openly proclaimed and pursued as the Way. Any degree of violent force up to and including genocide was publicly asserted to be correct as a means of implementing those policies.

It was an intolerable situation. Every filicide longs to practice his tyranny openly, to have his omnipotence publicly recognized and revered. But the smart tyrant learns to live with the necessary frustration of dissimulation and restraint. If he does not learn that lesson, his subjects may well rebel, leaving the tyrant with nothing to tyrannize. And here—in the middle of the twentieth century—the world filicidal patriarchy was presented with an undisguised, unashamed exercise of filicidal tyranny. The only possible response was unrestrained hatred of the Germans, the Italians, and the Japanese, the more so as it seemed they were actually succeeding—they were expanding their areas of control at an alarming rate.

Something clearly had to be done, and what was done was, as always in filicidal crises, war. It turned out to be war to the very brink of annihilation (Dachau, Coventry, Dresden, Hiroshima, Nagasaki). The fascists had thrown down the patriarchal gauntlet, in effect saying: *We rule and we rule absolutely because, like you, we have penises. But* we rule openly and without liberal pretense, which of course *means that we are bigger and better men than you.*

World War II is remembered with such fond nostalgia because the bad guys were so clearly delineated. In a conflict where the enemy is so satisfyingly monstrous, one is relieved of the burden of seeing the monster within oneself. The fascists were not monsters. They were only men and women who had dropped one of the filicidal masks—that of dissimulation.

113

Every society contains fascist elements, since every society requires some degree of centralization of power. A brief catalog of the characteristics of the typical fascist society will serve to point up the extent to which fascism is merely filicide gone public:

- *Racism.* The fascist, as a good filicide, cannot exist without an enemy. It is frequently helpful and efficient to use race as the identifying characteristic. The successes of the civil rights movement over the years indicate some lessening of this tendency in America. At the same time, we have seen a rise in resistance to immigration and in the widespread use of the term "alien" to designate immigrants.

- *Inequality.* A fascist society proceeds on the public recognition of inequality among humans. Women in Germany became breeding machines. We resist the Equal Rights Amendment.

- *Children.* The indoctrination of children politically is a world-wide phenomenon. It appears to be the unavoidable price we pay for the benefits of universal education. Every society offers additional indoctrination. The Nazis had the Nuremberg rallies. We have the Superbowl and the World Series. On a somewhat subtler level of indoctrination, the Nazis had Albert Speer. We have Skidmore, Owings, and Merrill. The triumphs of American advertising speak for themselves, perhaps most loudly every Saturday morning.

- *Uniforms.* A fascist society uses uniforms extensively to identify the members of its elite groups. Men now affect, world-wide, the standard Western patriarchal uniform, the business suit. Some classes of workers, for various reasons, do not wear the uniform. But notice that for burial all men are so outfitted. The degree of male entrapment in the masculine role is also indicated by the fact that, while women can now wear pants-based attire, men—irrationally and compulsively—continue to confine themselves in pants.

Fascism is thus an externalization of filicidal consciousness onto large-scale secular reality, much as Christianity was (and is) an externalization of the same consciousness onto large-scale religious reality. The filicidal analysis of political theory and practice can be extended with equally fruitful results to any nation, no matter what it's stated ideology may be. In Russia, for example, the state theoretically becomes the filicidal parent, but in practice the tendency has been always toward more or less overt father worship. Marxism represents an intelligent, sophisticated attempt to magnify the filicidal nuclear family to such an extent that the entire society becomes one family.

The Frankenstein myth is alive and well not just in America but around the world. Two recent works with surprising resonances from that myth will provide an indication of just how far we have come since we sat for our portrait by Mary Shelley.

HAL 9000

Where can we turn to find a coldness greater than that of Shelley's Arctic? Space. And who or what could we find to be a more nearly perfect son than Frankenstein's monster? A thinking machine. *2001: A Space Odyssey,* by Arthur C. Clarke and Stanley Kubrick, is one of the most revealing tellings of filicidal myth this century has produced. Hal, the thinking and talking computer in the movie, is the ultimate son: Frankenstein's monster perfected to such an extent that we see at last that it is not necessary to be sexual at all in order to be a successful filicidal entity.

Following initial critical puzzlement when the movie was first released, there came a slow about-face. The technological virtuosity of the special effects was enough to give anyone with a taste for futuristic verisimilitude pause for thought. Beneath that clever surface that Clarke and Kubrick had created—with the insufficiently acclaimed aid of Douglas Trumbull—lay much more. But what was it? Was it merely a sort of garbled metaphysic, or a profound religious statement? No one could say for sure, and with reserve worthy of zen masters, Clarke and Kubrick weren't talking. So each critic reached down into some long-neglected corner of his or her bag of esthetic tricks and pulled out his or her particular existential anchor for public display. "Unaccustomed as I am to religious exhibitionism" seemed to be the standard implicit disclaimer as each reviewer contemplated Kubrick's and Clarke's science fiction conundrum.

With a bit of esthetic-religious backing and filling we soon got *2001* safely filed away in a cultural pigeon hole marked *Religion: Subgroup Science and Technology,* and let it go at that. This pigeon hole does not contain too many other artifacts, but it is not far distant from one marked *Science: Subgroup Hubris and Destruction,* in which we had long ago filed away Mary Shelley's novel. Such a classification really was safe, or so it seemed. After all, it was only a movie and a science-fiction movie at that, so there was no need to get upset about it. Just as: Mary Shelley wrote a classic horror story, so what else is new?

·

2001 is a murder story. Five, possibly six, homicides occur. The first is in the pre-historic prologue. A group of starving humanoid apes on the African veldt encounter an extraterrestrial visitor in the form of a black monolith and have their consciousness changed from that of nonconceptualizing animals to that of conceptualizing humans. Result: the first tool-weapon. One of the apes toys with the dried bones left over from a long ago meal. Something clicks and the jawbone becomes a club with which to slaughter beast—and human, or what passes for human at the time. We see the first murder, and we watch the first murderer, drunk with the ecstasy of his new-found power and control, fling his weapon to the heavens.

The bone never descends, because as it floats toward the apogee of its parabolic flight, Kubrick cuts to a Pan American rocket drifting lazily through near space. It is an outrageously presumptuous cut, as if the moviemakers were saying: we let you see the beginning as it happened millions of years ago; and since all endings are contained in that beginning, whatever may have come between beginning and ending is so predictable as not to warrant examination. What follows in the movie is an end, but also a beginning.

Haywood Floyd, head of the American space program in 1997, is on a secret mission to the moon. An American team of scientists on the moon has discovered a large black monolith a few feet beneath the lunar surface. Dating of the moon soil in which it was buried indicates it has been there some three million years. We follow Floyd on his flight, as he first stops at the huge earth satellite where he encounters a group of curious Russian scientists whom he leaves as baffled about his mission as they were when he met them. After placing a birthday call to his young daughter on Earth, he boards another rocket and we journey moonward with him. After landing he attends a meeting at which all the scientists involved report their theories concerning the monolith. He goes to the site, arriving at lunar sunrise. As the rays of the sun strike the object it emits a massive burst of electromagnetic radiation.

Another cut brings us to the heart of the story. We are on board an enormous spaceship bound for Jupiter. The ship carries five men—Dave Bowman and Frank Poole, together with three scientists in a state of suspended animation—plus one rather extraordinary computer, the HAL 9000, who thinks, or who at least gives every indication that he thinks. Hal is referred to as "he" because of his name and the masculine voice with which his makers equipped him. There follows another dazzling technological sequence in which we become acquainted with life on board the *Discovery*. Dave and Frank quickly show themselves to be your traditional cool astronaut types, while Hal is hardly distinguishable from them except for the fact that he has no body as such. In a sense, the entire ship is Hal's body. He has sensors—audio, video, and other kinds—everywhere. Hal functions as just another member of the crew. He keeps tabs on the ship, monitors transmissions from Earth, chats with Dave and Frank, plays chess with them, interviews them concerning their mental attitude, and even offers constructive criticism of Dave's sketches of life on the ship.

The voyage proceeds uneventfully until Hal informs the astronauts that a crucial part of an antenna is about to malfunction. Frank leaves the ship and retrieves the module in question. Tests, run with Hal's assistance, reveal no potential trouble. Dave and Frank are puzzled. They inform Earth and Earth says they will look into the problem. Hal is puzzled too, or so he says. Then Hal informs them that the substitute module Frank had installed is about to malfunction. Dave and Frank get very worried and hold what they think is a secret conversation in which they decide they may have to disconnect Hal since they cannot trust him to run the ship if he is going to make mistakes such as this. Unknown to them Hal is reading their lips through one of his many television eyes.

Frank leaves the ship again to replace the module. At this point the second murder occurs (the first having been the murder of the apeman). Hal takes control of Frank's space pod and rams Frank with it, cutting his oxygen line and sending him hurtling off into space. With ultimate astronaut coolness Dave rushes to the rescue in another space pod. Too late. Frank is dead. Dave retrieves the body and returns to the ship only to find that Hal will not open the door to let him in. While Dave is trying to find a way into the ship, Hal cuts off the life support systems of the hibernating scientists—murders Three, Four, and Five. Dave jettisons Frank's body and uses an emergency hatch to re-enter the ship. He makes his way through the ship toward Hal's "brain." Hal asks him what he is doing. Dave does not speak. He enters the compartment containing "Hal" and begins disconnecting Hal's higher functions one by one. If we consider Hal human, this is the sixth murder.

Hal talks as Dave unplugs his mind. He says he is afraid. Dave does not respond. At the last, his voice failing, Hal tells us who he is and the date of his birth: he is H—A—L 9000, activated at Urbana, Illinois, January 12, 1992. He tells us his makers taught him a song. As he dies he sings the beginning of "A Bicycle Built for Two."

Cut to Dave, near Jupiter now, leaving the *Discovery* in a space pod. Whatever his purpose—and we never learn what it is—he is diverted by another of the monoliths floating nearby in space. Dave enters another dimension, something beyond our space-time, and after a fantastic journey, emerges in a suite of elegantly furnished rooms. Time there is hugely compressed. Dave leaves the pod and stumbles through the rooms. The pod is there, and then it is not. Dave ages rapidly. We see him, dressed in pajamas and robe, eating at a formally set table. Then his shriveled figure is lying on the bed, only his eyes show some sign of life. He raises his arm and points and we see that a monolith has appeared at the foot of the bed.

Cut to an embryo, seemingly human, in whose features those of Dave are vaguely discernible, floating in its placenta through space, approaching Earth. End.

117

The movie presents its story enigmatically, with large gaps left for the viewer to deal with on his or her own. The omissions are not the taunting, malicious, or careless kind used by certain other artistic explorers. The film contains more than enough information for any viewer willing to use his or her creative imagination to follow this modern Odysseus from home to home. The movie is also unusual in that long stretches go by with not a word on the soundtrack. For a culture as addicted to words as this one is (*pace,* McLuhan), a two and a half hour movie with only forty-five minutes of dialogue was an affront to our verbal sensibilities. Adding to the confusion surrounding the movie's initial reception was the fact that its major points are blatantly accentuated by emotionally loaded musical cues.

Time passed and *2001* eventually found an audience, even a very large audience, and picked up a passel of admiring critics along the way. Most of the critics nestled up quite cozily to the rather obvious scientific-intellectual-religious message which the surface of the movie presents.

The theory of filicide enables us to enter another level of the movie entirely. The portrait that Mary Shelley did of us has been proved more accurate than we might wish by the scientific and political belligerence since her day. Here, in *2001,* we have another portrait of our filicidal selves. As in Shelley, it is a peculiar kind of double rendering, like a cubist painting, showing more sides of a person than our orthodox vision is accustomed to seeing at one time.

What is it that causes Hal, the perfect son, to commit murder? As Dave is unplugging Hal's mind, an automatic sequence triggers the playing of a video tape. From that tape Dave learns for the first time that the mission is not a simple voyage of exploration to Jupiter but is a result of the finding of the monolith on the moon—the radio signals the monolith had emitted were aimed at Jupiter. So Hal had known all along what the trip was really about but had been instructed to lie to Dave and Frank about it. In other words, Hal had been filicidally acculturated by his human fathers and mothers.

But the proto-scene for Hal had not yet occurred. Hal functioned beautifully as a bodyless human, manipulating and controlling with superb, emotionless precision and reliability. But the seed of deceit had been planted. As mysteriously as Cain was moved to kill Abel, Hal is moved, for reasons he can no more admit to himself than we have been able to admit the realities behind our filicidal violence to ourselves, to deceive his brothers-fathers-sons about the antenna. Which produces the proto-scene when he reads Dave's and Frank's lips as they decide to murder him. Hal, acting in the grand tradition of filicidal humanity, responds in kind.

2001 presents a portrait of humanity even more intensely filicidal than that in *Frankenstein.* Its focus is relentlessly patriarchal. We are put in a world without women, without children, without warmth. We move in a world where everything is literally *man*made, including this grotesque ultimate Son of Man: Hal, my son the murderer. Shelley set the key scenes of her story in a world of ice. *2001* is played out in the realm of absolute zero. What are we to read in this but an externalization of the emotional freeze of the human nuclear family? Here we find the perfect realization of the metaphor for filicide as not literally murder but as a kind of freezing, a making-rigid of large areas of our organic potential.

Shelley ended with despair. *2001* ends with hope. Hal is us and we are Hal. But we are also more. We create Hal—just as we create Adam, and Cain, and Oedipus, and Orestes, and Jesus, and Hamlet, and Frankenstein's monster in our own image. They are what we think we are and they are also what we become. But we are always more, as *2001* shows us.

Dave, the last homicide, himself dies at the hand, or under the aegis, of agencies beyond his comprehension. He dies only to find that death is not what filicidal humanity has made it out to be. If death is not what it seems to our filicidal selves, then what are we to make of our lives? It seems that we have constructed our brutally controlled and controlling selves partly on the poor bargain that the filicidal family forces on us. We have also externalized the politics of that family onto the politics of nature itself—including death, the result being that we come to see all existence as a very poor bargain. Trying to make the best of it, we strike this pose: *All right, Death, you may have me at the end but until then, I am the captain of my fate etc., and I'll run this little ship of mine any way I please, giving full vent to my little boy's/little girl's frustration at the mockery which you will make of my grandest achievements.* If death turns out to be more than end, more even than judgment by the biggest father of them all, the filicidal self must at that point find itself in somewhat of a quandary.

2001 is to *Frankenstein* as Goethe's *Faust* is to Marlowe's *Doctor Faustus.* Marlowe's hubristic philosopher ends in eternal damnation. Two hundred years later Goethe, dealing with the same material, was able to realize the possibility of mercy and forgiveness at the end of Faust's troubled life. Shelley's filicidal scientist plunges unerringly toward despair and death. One hundred and fifty years later Kubrick and Clarke, dealing with the same myth, give us a transcendental astronaut who undergoes the filicidally heretical experience of rebirth.

The vision of *2001,* for all its scope, remains flawed. The movie carries our filicidal behavior to the point where we create the perfect son. The humans around him seem almost pitiable so imperfect are they in comparison to him. But what has happened at the end is that—once again—an agency of external, parental redemption so characteristic of the filicidal mind has been shifted up one dimension. The monolith, whatever it represents, is only a scientific rendering of God the Father who saves or damns for reasons of his own. Monolith knows best. So once again we see ourselves seeking salvation by means of some grandiose power external to ourselves—a continuation of the endless quest to recapture that forgotten time long ago when father's yes was heaven, and his no, hell.

MYRA BRECKINRIDGE

Myra Breckinridge is Wyatt Earp in drag, the ultimate put-down and put-on of filicidal humanity. She's a two-breasted, dildoe-toting hermaphroditic Amazon whose goal is nothing less than total "power over both sexes and, yes, even over life itself." Her mission as she states it is:

> the destruction of the last vestigial traces of traditional manhood in the race in order to realign the sexes, thus reducing the population while increasing human happiness and preparing for the next stage.

Myra Breckinridge is America and her failure is the failure of this country's naive belief in its ability to control everything benignly and benevolently. She is Yankee ingenuity carried to its extreme, rigorously logical conclusion: if the world is not the way you like it, change it with whatever degree of force is necessary, but do it cleverly and with style. American tyranny at home and American imperialism abroad have succeeded so well because they are the tyranny and imperialism of panache, elan, and chutzpah. The American contribution to that process known as history has consisted of making filicide palatable. What our filicidal gods needed all along, it turns out, was a good public relations man and a well-trained, smooth-talking traveling salesman. Recapturing something of the lost vision of the ancient matriarchy, Gore Vidal at last gives America its savior—a male lesbian transsexual. Myra Breckinridge is a nonalcoholic Willie Loman who knows the value of Dale Carnegie. She is Werner Erhard with a sense of irony. In her willful, stylish attempt to rearrange the sexual priorities of an entire civilization we see reflected in a bizarre and even obscene way the end of American innocence. In God we trusted for over three hundred years, but it turned out to be not a god who had made us in his image but one whom we had made in our own image. In *Myra Breckinridge* our chicken-hearted, blustering bravado comes home to roost. The novel contains a mythic acting-out of why we were in Vietnam (with harmonics produced and resonances sounded far beyond Mailer's hearing) and why we withdrew from that rape before coming—a mythic acting-out of the nightmare side of the American Dream in its most basic and bloody essentials.

Myra Breckinrdige yields up the last insight into the nature of filicidal behavior. She is a one-person nuclear family. In her polymorphous self she embodies and acts out all the roles: mother, father, husband, wife, son, daughter, brother, sister. Myron

Breckinridge fucks himself. The offspring of that incestuous and bloody union is Myra Breckinridge. Myron is thus Myra's husband and father and brother and son. And Myra is Myron's wife and mother and sister and daughter. Myron/Myra is a Victor Frankenstein who creates the monster directly out of himself. And we see at last that filicide is an on-going, internal process. Whatever agents may be involved in the original incident of filicide, however neatly we may isolate initial filicide in a proto-scene, filicide must finally be seen as an internal event.

The force and habit of tradition, along with the supportive filicidal input we get from our families and friends and the society, lend great sustaining impetus to our filicidal behavior. But each individual's continuation in the old ways is—if the concept of adult responsibility means anything at all—finally a matter of choice. We are all Myron and Myra Breckinridge. Each of us is a walking nuclear family. So thoroughly have we learned the filicidal lessons and imperatives that we have internalized the roles completely. As an adult, I am my father and my mother, my husband and my wife, my son and my daughter, my brother and my sister. Like Myron and Myra Breckinridge, I shift quickly—though not entirely without pain—from role to role in my incessant search for absolute power over both sexes and indeed over life itself.

Myron Breckinridge knows and lives the failure of modern masculinity. Then he emasculates himself, has his breasts pumped full of silicone and his veins filled with hormone shots—and lives out the failure of modern femininity. Myra, with an almost mystical vision (her great insight is: "Nothing is what it seems and what nothing seems is false") and with a genuinely mythical fervor, sets out to become Woman Triumphant, the new Magna Mater, Kali incarnate, only to have her best-laid, rationally calculated plans reduce her to a man again—such is her tragedy—who plays out an empty life of mock masculinity in the suburban wasteland of California. Filicide, and with it, history, begins and ends at home.

Before George Washington was, Myra Breckinridge is.

122

III. THE FILICIDAL PRESENT

There is a reality here whose form, quality, and values are such that one seeks to avoid it if at all possible. Our alacrity in avoiding it is very much a part of the history humanity has written of itself. Even when we brush up against it as we have done here, we still want to look the other way, still want to embrace the old, comfortable idealisms.

Filicide is only another name for barbarism. Or perhaps: a grotesquely civilized kind of barbarism. Shelley—one always gets back to her—seems to have said, if not everything, at least a great deal more than we wanted to hear. The self-hatred which came gurgling briefly to the surface when Frankenstein disposed of the body of his still-born daughter is a powerful clue to what is still hidden.

The perverted homoeroticism of the violently enforced masculine exclusivity of the entire civilization makes a mockery of the best we have done and accomplished. Behind the glorious friezes of Greece, the splendid moral temples of Israel, the monumental architecture of Egypt, the serpentine mysteries of the Orient, the managerial mastery of Rome, the beauty of Catholic ritual, the flowering of Renaissance creativity, and our own modern polymath exploration of intellectual creativity—behind that rich facade of civilized progress lies the personal and social dynamic of filicide. In this civilization the public face of filicide is patriarchal. We have killed our sons to keep the parade going. It is a show whose details and sweep we know well. Even now we would say: *Yes, we have done that to ourselves to create—however bloodily and slowly—a better world for everyone.* But what do we see if we look behind the facade of patriarchal history?

For one thing, we see a small but highly visible group of males—heretics, deviants, outsiders—who for one reason or another chose not to participate directly in the deadly pursuit of ever greater filicidal control. One of the gaps in our almost perfect filicidal armor consists in the fact that at the same time that we were creating a planetary civilization based on the goal of total control, we, perhaps inadvertently, perhaps not, left sufficient growing room for some of our male number to explore various heretical, nonfilicidal lives. We have usually dealt harshly with such men when their activities became public knowledge and formed a threat to the ongoing larger system of filicidal values. But those male renegades have existed in each generation, and still exist today. Men willing to pay the price have had a certain freedom open to them.

If we look behind the same historical facade for female renegades, we find almost nothing. Here and there we see a woman rising by means of almost incredible abilities above the orthodox female role to explore for a time her human potential outside that role. Otherwise the record is bare. The ancient thoroughness of filicidal sexism makes a mockery of the best of the lives of men.

What we have created is a barbarian civilization, in which generation after generation of masculine masters brutally competed with each other to be king of the mountain and brutally raised generation after generation of sons in the same stultifying pattern, while at the same time we confined all women to one role, that of caretaker-mother. It is barbaric slavery of an order and a magnitude so great that it is beyond comprehension. Open a history of Western art, of Western science, religion or whatever, and consider what you find there: an inverted world of pervertedly asexual homoeroticism. Having excluded women from our lives except as doting, obedient, helpmeet slaves, we march through the pages of history masturbating in front of each other, saying in effect: *Look at this tool! Look what I can do!* And we stand around applauding, urging each other on, to see who can come the farthest, the longest, and the most.

In the past century and a half women have begun to speak of their oppression and to act to free themselves. As long as the documentation of our patriarchal oppression has come from women and has concerned what we have done to women, we could, in our best paternal way, nod sagely and set right the obvious wrongs. Everybody is in favor of equal pay for equal work. We can even feel self-righteous about our efforts to right certain obvious wrongs because in our divinely ordained onanistic glory we can easily understand how other humans might want very much to be equal to *us*. That self-serving masculine response to the insights of feminism is based on a very limited perception of those insights.

The theory of filicide makes it possible to see the hollowness and the often lethal reality of both sex roles. The theory undercuts the last possible defense of historical masculinity by revealing that at the same time that we were committing gynocide, we were also committing filicide, which is to say homicide, which is to say suicide.

The heart of the feminist movement is based on a questioning of the most basic values of the civilization. The theory of filicide offers a framework in which women are no longer defined in terms of their oppression by men, and in which men are no longer defined in terms of their oppression of women. The feminist framework already gives women a largely adequate framework within which to examine and alter their lives in any number of healthy ways. The theory of filicide—at the same time that it speaks directly to women—offers men a similar framework within which to begin questioning the values we use to create our own human lives. What we see in Western myth is a profound, continuing, and intensifying alienation of men from themselves, from women, and from the organic world of natural process and growth. Our basic mental attitude—control—and our basic emotional stance—repression—are both founded on an alienation from our male bodies, our male minds, and our human souls. The alienation reaches its most extreme development in heterosexual men, who will—when their fear has begun to subside—have a great deal to learn from homosexual men.

Toughness is the central criterion of manhood, as we have lived that role historically. We kept telling the story in different ways, finding all sorts of mythic and religious justifications for our destructive behavior. Whoever or whatever Jesus was, we killed him twice over. Once on the cross and then soon afterwards by making him into an image of our own filicidal selves. Whatever his message may have been it was poisoned by the vicious Pauline interpretation which, along with the confused and contradictory accounts of the gospel writers, provided perfect justification for the countless murders and wars we have since carried out in the name of the Son of God.

What we did in Jesus' name we did as functionaries and members of "his" church. We were thus provided with a certain anonymity and avoidance of individual responsibility similar to the stronger sense of mythic reality one perceives in the records of Greek and Jewish experience. In *Hamlet* we found the first sketch of the individual, secularized male soul wrestling with the chains of filicidal tyranny as they extend from beyond the grave. In *Frankenstein* the problem was at last outlined free of institutional connections and rationalizations. There we saw father meet son in a duel to the death. *2001* displayed the reduction of filicidal man to machine. And in *Myra Breckinridge* we saw how the four-character absurdist drama known as the nuclear family exists and operates within each person.

The theory of filicide makes clear the fact that all those portraits of seemingly diverse men through the ages are portraits of the same person—the son striving to be the father striving to be the son striving to be the father, etc. Neither the pettiness nor the naivity of our masculine humanity can any longer serve as a justification or excuse for our massive and ancient barbarism. Here, we arrive back at the painting with which we began. The "great martyrdom" to which Lovis Corinth refers is that of historical masculinity, historical man, all of us, famous or not, mythic or not. We are martyrs to ourselves and the mutilated bodies and souls of the women and children are nowhere to be seen.

Crucifixion: because it is the most effective public splaying and displaying of the body masculine. A protracted and painful public death worthy of the self-hatred which produces such a bloody act.

Crucifixion: because it is near-perfect humilation. The king is reduced to total and highly visible impotence.

Crucifixion: because it is the most dramatic and prolonged of executions. A theatrical externalization of the reality of filicide, a prolongation of life under terrible conditions, a life which is no life which is centered on death.

Filicide: the crucifixion of self as child, the fixing of the self onto the cross of traditional childhood.

8. CHILDREN

The theory of filicide reveals the limitations of two kinds of solutions on which we have relied when presented with social problems. Ideological solutions have been thoroughly contaminated by the unrecognized filicidal behavior of those proposing the solutions. A common example is the socialist revolution that quickly and smoothly turns into dictatorship. Similarly, legal solutions, no matter how insightful, rapidly degenerate to the lowest common denominator of unrecognized filicide operating in the society. Compare, for example, the ideals of political constitutions with the filicidal practice of those constitutions.

In a sense, the anarchist is the only person who has some perception of the filicidal limitations and attempts to act accordingly. But the anarchist, having failed to discriminate violences, easily falls into the ideological trap. Hence the common sight of the anarchist turned physically violent terrorist, or behaviorally violent guru.

The theory indicates finally, in a convincing manner, that we are to rely on our own solutions. To investigate the experience of our fellow creatures and to compare it with our own is one thing. Too often such investigation only lends support to our filicidal quest for quasi-parental or pseudo-parental solutions from an agent outside ourselves. Close attention to the lives of filicidal heretics is certainly in order. But the theory of filicide makes clear the kind of result which deification of those heretics always brings: more violence.

What, then, of the children?

They are excluded, legally, morally, behaviorally, religiously, philosophically, politically, from the process of social creation. That exclusion is one of the two marks of true slavery. The other: children are also excluded from the process of self-creation. The successful child is the one who most skillfully and quickly constructs

129

its personality to conform to the smothering confines of the traditional mold of masculinity or femininity. Where is hope for the child? Occasionally the child may come across an adult who is in some way growing beyond the filicidal mold. The child may think: *When I grow up, I can do that. I can be like that.* Otherwise the experience of childhood, even as we adults preen our liberated and liberating selves and strut before one another wearing the feathers of our sagelike pride, remains bleak and ominous, played out on a dark landscape littered with brightly colored toys and forgotten dreams.

Filicide will continue unabated as long as the legal systems of planetary civilization continue to support universally the ancient belief that parents own children. The most humanitarian possible social act, indeed in a sense the only genuinely humanitarian act now left to us as historical creatures, is to relinquish ownership of the children. Our "ownership" is after all only another of those large pretenses with which we have from the beginning of history shored up our shaky filicidal selves and our equally shaky reality.

To let the children go. That does not mean to evict them forcibly or any such nonsense. It means only to create opportunities for them where they may safely and freely explore their potential without the constant threat of adult, filicidal intervention. Filicidal heretics have left behind a goodly number of hints and rough maps concerning how to proceed in that direction. It is a direction of interest not only to children but to adults as well. The exploration of which we speak here is that of the human soul which we have managed to imprison rather neatly in its childhood manifestation, not realizing that we have thereby also neatly imprisoned our adult souls. The search here, then, is for a way to escape the eternal recurrence of historical damnation.

Though we may disagree politically about the right of every adult to the basics of sustenance and shelter, the planetary civilization is pretty much in agreement now that every child has those rights simply by the fact of its existence. If we add to that the right to full protection under the law against physical or behavioral violence, then we have the beginning of a foundation for a society in which we can let the children go.

That is the most humanitarian act open to us now because the children cannot rise in rebellion against us. We *are* bigger and stronger and we are all furthermore in agreement that we do own the children. To free the children is an act of mercy, of benevolence, of trust, of hope. It is an act to put an end to the real source of colonialism, of exploitation, and of contrived violence—the imperialism of the souls of children. The only pressure on us, urging us to let the children go, is internal. No external agent is at hand to force us to do it. It can be done only by adults acting from the filicidally heretical belief in their own ultimate goodness—and that of the children.

Let us examine a hypothetical example. Suppose the child's right to sustenance, shelter, and protection against physical and behavioral violence were law. A child could knock at any door and, barring unusual circumstances, expect entry, food, and shelter. Any violence against the child would be dealt with as the most serious and heinous of crimes. That such a suggestion should sound outrageous is a measure of the depth of our immersion in filicide: *Surely such freedom for children would produce a generation of wastrels who would never learn the value of work,* etc. Perhaps. Perhaps we would also produce a generation of adults who would see how we have created a world in which we bewail and punish the idlers, the malcontents, the criminals, and the insane, while we remain blissfully unaware that our bewailing and punishing (which we think of as being the essence of civilized behavior) is at least as violent and destructive as any of the behavior which we bewail and punish.

The magnitude of both historical and contemporary filicide is such that it is unlikely that any conceivable corrective measures would be excessive. We are speaking here of an end to a system of slavery as old as history. An end to slavery is a beginning of freedom. In such a situation work and play tend to become more or less indistinguishable. The unthinkable happens: the child learns to work, the adult learns to play.

Child labor is nightmarish only in a world where adult labor is nightmarish. Compulsory miseducation of children will continue as long as the accepted and applauded model for adult behavior is compulsory success, which in its organismic and societal effects is in fact compulsory failure. Education, as A. S. Neill put it, is a matter of freedom, not license. In a filicidal society we think of freedom as something guaranteed by an outside agency, a set of laws with interpretors and enforcers (judges and police). Beyond filicide, freedom is that state in which one accepts the responsibility for one's acts. It is there that a life begins so different from this one that we now can only glimpse it in our puzzling dreams which come to us every night and which we have learned so efficiently to forget every morning.

9. The Paradox of Nonviolent Action

The desperate willingness with which we historically have embraced a life after death as reward for this death in life is one of the strongest pieces of evidence supporting the theory of filicide. We know we do not live, not really, so we construct myths to account for our death in life and to provide hope for release and reward. At the center of the myths we place the suffering child. Our filicidal dream is that the child rises again after death. That an image of a son's bloody death on a cross should have become a central symbol of our civilization indicates something of the extremity of our predicament.

We have the word, the concept, the myth, and the vision to express that dream: resurrection. Strangely, we do not have the word which logically would be used to express the first rising, the one that precedes this re-rising depicted in the central myth. That word, properly, would be: surrection. Perhaps the fact that we do not have that word is another of those strange instances of hidden knowledge contained within the language. If our birth is not a true birth but only a birth into death, then birth is not a proper surrection—so, naively, we do not bother with the word.

Rational analysis is an efficient, effective way of dealing with immediate problems of physical survival, as science and technology have demonstrated. We have been so impressed by the solutions to survival problems generated by science and technology that we have mistakenly assumed that the way of knowledge on which they are based, that of rational analysis, is adequate and sufficient for all other problems.

Rational analysis has two basic values:

- Survival value, and
- Play value.

The usefulness of rational analysis is, in fact, radically limited to the so-called physical realm. Once we have established ourselves with a modicum of security and comfort in that realm by means of science and technology, rational analysis ceases to have critical, essential value. To the extent that we then attempt to force solutions of nonphysical problems by means of rational analysis, that way of knowledge itself becomes dangerous and destructive.

To use Lawrence LeShan's perceptive terminology: rational analysis is a great help in finding solutions to *structural* problems—understanding why it is easier to pull a large piece of wood if it has wheels attached than if it doesn't. But rational analysis is a great hindrance in dealing with *functional* problems—traditional psychoanalysis did not cure anything, it only made it possible for a patient to accept certain fears and insecurities as normal.

Beyond the point where physical security and comfort are attained, rational analysis has at most play value. The problem of filicide cannot be solved by rational analysis. Rational analysis can do no more than demonstrate the existence and nature of the problem. We cannot stop controlling by controlling more, or better, or differently.

To return to the resurrection metaphor: how can we "rise again" if we have not yet risen the first time? Why should we die twice to be born once?

That dilemma brings us to paradox. Western civilization has steadfastly refused to employ tools other than rational analysis over the long term. Language, which is to say, symbol manipulation in all its forms, has been our chief tool for rational analysis. As our desire for control has intensified, so has our use of that tool. Along the way we have experimented with other tools. For several centuries we tried out the many devices of religion, with mixed results. For several centuries we tried the many devices of art, also with mixed results. And we still have those tools with us, though we now use them either for sporadic solace needed in times of crisis, or for entertainment.

We have refined our discrimination of violences in this peculiar progress called history largely as a result of a long sequence of rational analyses. Historically, two reactions to analysis of our ways of violence may be discerned. The one encompasses that set of attitudes called "conservative." Those persons have tended to resist rational analysis and have opted for the status quo, with a strong tendency to defend the status quo in either religious or social-elitist terms. Those who have welcomed rational analysis have tended to do so with as much force as have those who resist it. These persons display a wide set of attitudes called "liberal." Their behavior frequently produces political revolution. The point is that both the political right and the political left are implicated in the ongoing violence which characterizes history.

As has become clear, the entire process of acculturation to which we subject children is a series of interferences, so many acts of violence committed on the children. But the end of our filicidal analysis also yielded up the insight that filicide is finally an internal act of violence. Thus any overt, social response—however well-intentioned—is, paradoxically, itself only another filicidal act of violence.

Dismissing out of hand the value of that adolescent foolishness known as existential paralysis, we are then left to learn the discrimination of filicidal violences. At first glance, we seem to find ourselves in a double-bind. We are damned if we act, and we are damned if we don't. But notice what happens if we consider the classic double-bind situation in the light of the theory of filicide. The exquisite pain we derive from any existential double-bind is only a masochistic variation on the basic filicidal theme of control: the individual attempts to escape responsibility for his or her own actions by demonstrating rationally that all action is at best foolish and at worst tragically painful. Notice that these two possibilities are only philosophical reformulations of the two basic myths—Orestes with his tragic success, and Oedipus with his tragic failure. Such a double-bind is possible only for a creature so intent on absolute, perfect answers that he or she is blinded to all other possible ways of knowing. The fact that we cannot avoid violence no matter what we do is a fact that the absolutist, writhing in the wondrous pain of success/failure, is unwilling to accept. Yet, paradoxically, that fact provides a way out of the filicidal, acculturative conundrum—or at least points toward a way out.

It is likely that filicide, pretty much in the form we have it today, is going to be with us for quite some time. As always—whether we recognize it or not—our only choice will continue to be at what level of violence we choose to exist. It would be easy to create a filicidal ideology, actually an anti-filicidal ideology—a program of necessary and desirable reforms of society and the family in order to end the brutality that children experience. One point for such a program is the idea of letting the children go. For most people that would be a dangerously threatening suggestion. Other, far more threatening examples spring readily to mind, the most potent of course being the reform of child-rearing in such a way that children would be overtly sexual from a very early age, both among themselves and with adults. The day when these and many other reforms are realized is inevitable. To demand such changes now would itself be rape of the most primitive kind—rape of the minds of millions of concerned, well-intentioned, loving parents who are very frightened and very confused in their own lives and who are rearing classically frightened and confused filicidal children.

Both the revolutionary and the reactionary find it possible to act bloodily and to justify their actions through an extreme form of identification with various patterns of violence. The revolutionary has an answer to the world's problems and attempts to make the world over into that answer. The reactionary finds the status quo pleasantly worthwhile and strives mightily to defend it. One of the pitfalls in the process of discriminating violences is the construction of one's personality in such a way that the personality comes to equate itself with the very act of discrimination.

So we take the process of perception one step farther and call it "apperception." Apperception may be understood as doubly removed self-consciousness. Put another way, it is thinking thinking about thinking. It is a nonjudgmental rendering of the self in all its facets, both violent and nonviolent. We arrive again at paradox: it is the self observed and—another Western heresy—not interfered with. (The Heisenberg Principle is only an externalization of filicidal violence down to the quantum realm.)

In both East and West this kind of apperception, attainable and useful though it is, has more often than not degenerated into an abdication of individual responsibility. We retain the form, unaware of the inner vacuity. The range of empty, once magical gesture proceeds from the simplistic phenomenon of so-called prayer by television evangelists, through the somewhat more complex structures and poses of the various filicidal religions, to the thoughtful, troubled ascetic who physically withdraws from contact with society.

●

Our acts may or may not have meaning. Or they may occur and exist in such a way that they simultaneously have meaning and do not have meaning. Or in such a way that they neither have meaning nor do not have meaning. The very high energy levels involved in any act of physical or mental violence obscure the act and its echoes so thoroughly that questions concerning whether any of our acts have meaning or not are little more than clever pastimes for anorganic minds. Yet is that not always, always the question behind all questions: does my pain matter?

Each answers that question explicitly or implicitly with a life. And each answer is different. Both the revolutionary and the reactionary answer with a loud "Yes!" The reactionary says: *Yes, my pain matters but there is nothing I can do about it now so I am acting in such a way as to make it stop when I retire or when I die.* The revolutionary says: *Yes, my pain matters and I am acting in such a way as to make it stop either now or very soon.*

●

The sixty-third chapter of the *Tao Te Ching* begins with the radical suggestion:

wei wu wei

the literal meaning of which is:

action not action.

135

Action without action. Action without interference, without violence. Language resists such heresy. One translator tried: *to act in repose*—which conjures up images of carefree billionaires pushing buttons in Las Vegas penthouses, or timeworn Tibetan yogis pulling telepathic strings from Himalayan caves.

To act without acting. To interfere without interfering. Analysis stops here because it cannot deal with the paradoxical possibility of control without controlling. And we are left—not with silence, but with laughter. In the distance the attentive ear hears the oh-so-gently mocking, always encouraging sound of laughter from the eternal mystery of grace.